DEC 15 1961

THE CINQUE PORTS

1 "DOST THOU KNOW DOVER?" "AY, MASTER"

King Lear, Act IV, Sc. 1

SHAKESPEARE CLIFF

THE
CINQUE PORTS

Ronald and Frank
Jessup

WITH A FOREWORD
BY
ELIZABETH BOWEN

B. T. BATSFORD LTD
LONDON *and* NEW YORK

First Published, 1952

Made and printed in Great Britain by
THE WHITEFRIARS PRESS LTD., London and Tonbridge,
for the publishers B. T. BATSFORD, LTD.
LONDON : 15 North Audley Street, W.1, and Malvern Wells, Worcestershire.
NEW YORK : 122 East 55th St.   TORONTO : 103 St. Clair Avenue West.
SYDNEY : 156 Castlereagh Street.

CONTENTS

ACKNOWLEDGMENT

MAJOR M. TEICHMAN DERVILLE, O.B.E., D.L., J.P., F.S.A., a Coronation Baron and lately Speaker of the Ports, and the Registrar of the Cinque Ports, Mr. James A. Johnson, Town Clerk of Dover, have given special assistance to the Authors for which they are most grateful.

The Authors and Publishers express their thanks to the following photographers whose work is reproduced in this book:—

T. Edmondson for Figs. 17, 35 and 52 ; A. F. Kersting, F.R.P.S., for Figs. 9, 14, 19–22, 30, 31 and 45 ; Lambert Weston & Son Ltd., Dover, for Figs. 1, 4, 12, 13 and 32 ; The Mustograph Agency for Figs. 23, 24, 28, 29 and 42 ; H. S. Newcombe, F.R.P.S., for Figs. 8, 10, 18, 26, 33, 34, 36–8, 40 and 47–9 ; John H. Stone for Fig. 39 ; E. W. Tattersall for Figs. 27, 41 and 43 ; R. H. Windsor for Fig. 25 ; Reece Winstone, A.R.P.S., for Figs. 44, 50 and 51 ; the Executors of the late Richard Wyndham for Fig. 7.

The Map of East Kent and Figs. 2 and 46 are by R. F. Jessup. Figs. 3, 6 and 11 are from *The Times.*

For permission to adapt his Map of Romney Marsh the authors thank Dr. W. V. Lewis.

Fig. 2 is from Francis Sandford, *History of the Coronation of James II, etc.,* 1687.

Fig. 5 is from William Darell, *History of Dover Castle,* 1786.

The illustrations of the Brasen Horn and the Badge of the Ports were very kindly supplied by Major Teichman Derville.

LIST OF ILLUSTRATIONS

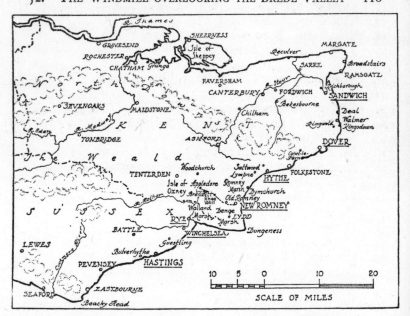

THE CINQUE PORTS AND THEIR PRINCIPAL MEMBERS

FOREWORD

By ELIZABETH BOWEN

THIS book on the Cinque Ports is a blend of portraiture with history, a picture of yesterday in the frame of to-day. The past of these places is of a length out of all proportion with their visible size; a particular glory has not so much departed as contracted into what for many people is little more than a legend, the rumour or ghost of a memory. Hastings, Dover, Sandwich, Romney and Hythe enshrine and honour their joint histories; yet it appears that outside the region these have remained, so far, little known. The names of the actual Cinque Ports are sometimes wrongly given; corporate or non-corporate members under their Charters are incorrectly promoted into their ranks, or confusion exists as to their relation with Winchelsea and Rye, the two Ancient Towns. As to fact, it has been the undertaking of this book's authors to enlighten us. But they do, as they have intended to do, more: they have evoked the atmosphere, revivified the excitement of centuries in which England first, as a power, began to be.

To-day only Dover is a functioning port; only Dover and Hastings, with her sea front, either show growth or claim any forward position in contemporary life. Sandwich, Romney and Hythe, together with Winchelsea and Rye, conduct, with varying vigour, their own existences, attracting the visitor and attaching the resident who finds himself subject to their peculiar charm. Behind the rise then decline, *as* ports, of four of the five, and the recession from maritime prominence of the Ancient Towns, is to be traced the slow drama of a changing coastline. The determining factor has been physical. Indeed, as the authors demonstrate, few parts of the coast of England could offer a more ideal study for the historical geographer than does this, of Sussex and Kent, with its layer upon layer of extinct, eroded or shrunken civilisations.

Roman then Norman enterprise had as its footing a conformation so much altered now that one reconstructs it only by an effort of mind—nor had there not been change between those two epochs. Stability, in Plantagenet times, was a fiction which study could have exposed; to that fiction the Cinque Ports owed their instatement, and to it their fast-growing importance and likely future were pinned, as it seemed, once for all.

The majestic, relentless war conducted by Nature against the Cinque Ports, and their defeat in it, could make melancholy reading, did there not stand out their triumphant human survival as institutions. As such, they were more than a local force; the extent of their dominance over sea and land was significant in the time which saw its height, has left its mark on all time, and, moreover, preserves itself in rights, ceremonies, procedures and exercises of jurisdiction which have not, and will never, become unmeaning, nominal or purely archaic. The joint history and individual stories of the Cinque Ports, with those of the Ancient Towns, are set out in pages now to come; it is not for a Foreword to either resume or anticipate. Ronald and Frank Jessup detail for us the constitutional framework within which the Cinque Ports, the Ancient Towns, and their subsidiaries, under their Charters, in and by virtue of their association, continue to act to-day. On the corporate and non-corporate members there has not, in this present volume, been room to more than touch: sensing unused material in abundance one is left hoping for further from these pens. Of the whole, the present-day setting is territorial—far away are the years when the Cinque Ports, by fulfilling their undertaking to man and send to sea all ships needful for the king's service, founded the Royal Navy. It was in return for this that reciprocal privileges were granted.

The authors, as topographers and archæologists, could have kept to being no more than informative. It is a gain, however, that they do also address themselves to feeling (though never to sentiment) and to the visual imagination. By nature we enter more deeply into the stories of places we either know well or have been caused to see. As it stands, this book is equally fit to go to those familiar with Hastings, Dover, Romney, Sandwich, Hythe, Winchelsea and Rye, and to those who know

2 CORONATION OF JAMES II, 1685 : Cinque Port Barons
bearing the Queen's canopy

3 THE GRAND COURT OF SHEPWAY : installation of the Rt. Hon. Winston
Churchill as Lord Warden, 1946

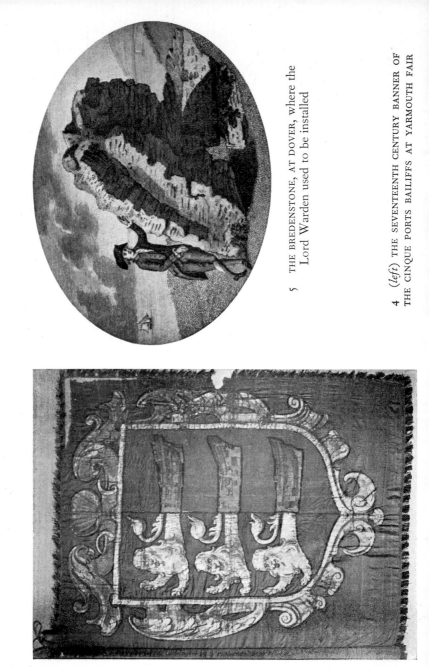

5 THE BREDENSTONE, AT DOVER, where the Lord Warden used to be installed

4 (*left*) THE SEVENTEENTH CENTURY BANNER OF THE CINQUE PORTS BAILIFFS AT YARMOUTH FAIR

14

them only by name. By the former, the evocation will be approved; for the latter it cannot, I imagine, fail to project pictures. The somnolent beauty of landlocked Romney; Sandwich's steep-roofed streets lit by estuarial gleams; the changing light over Hythe, with its great Marsh vista, on its forehead of hill—all these are conjured up; and not less so Dover's strange blend of the utilitarian, military and romantic. Old Hastings, still in essence aloof from the flourishing resort which shares its name, stands out in words, if still more in the photographs. Winchelsea, Rye reveal, to instructed vision, something more than their almost too evident picturesqueness. In all cases, there is direction of the eye to architecture and (more easily overlooked) the original plans and surviving structural features of towns once bound and now lost to the sea.

The Cinque Ports, and the whole belt of coastal country in which they stand, have an endemic temperament: something salt and sturdy about the very set of the bricks and stones, something vital about the surrounding contours—whether stretching flats, sweeping slopes, jutting heights. The people—race inside the English race—have, too, a character bred of their unique heritage, forged all the more perhaps by change and necessity. Of the many who care for this region, who seek or are haunted by it, few know it so thoroughly as these brother-authors—who are in fact authorities. Sons of Kent, out of a long heredity, these two are also linked in research. This adds unusual range and palpable substance to what is above all a labour of love.

CHAPTER I

THE BACKGROUND OF HISTORY

ON a clear day, looking eastwards across the English Channel from the Leas at Folkestone or from the fine stretch of greensward above the chalk cliffs at Capel-le-Ferne, you can plainly see the coast of France—the coast of France that is also the coast of the continent of Europe. Especially on a summer evening, when the setting sun illuminates, with a mysterious and pre-Raphaelite particularity, that far shore which is both familiar and foreign, you are likely to find yourself meditating, as many previous generations must have done, upon the changing fortunes in Britain's relations with Europe. On such occasions a train of questions present themselves. How real is that barrier formed by the twenty-mile wide Channel? Are we part of Europe, or do we stand aloof from her? Do we share with her a common culture, or is ours insular and peculiar? Do we follow where Europe has led, or are the roles reversed? And, sometimes at the back of the mind, sometimes in the forefront, the perennial question, is it to be peace or war?

To Kent and Sussex, stretching out like a hand—or a fist—towards France and the Low Countries, the question of peace or war has always been of immediate and intimate pertinence. For in peace the south-coast corner has been England's gateway to the continent; through it have passed, in both directions, kings, ambassadors, prelates, refugees, scholars, thieves, merchants, tourists—and ideas. And in war (all our major wars have been threats from the continent delivered mainly from France and Flanders) Kent and Sussex have stood as Britain's bastion, jutting out, pugnaciously defensive, towards hostile shores. From that remote time in prehistory when these islands became separated from the European mainland until this present year of 1951, which is perhaps witnessing the birth-throes of some kind of union of Western Europe, no other theme in our history offers the same persistent grandeur and interest as the problem of Britain's relations with the continent.

It is, in the main, to their situation confronting the European mainland that the towns of the Kent and Sussex coast owe their early importance. But during the last century and a half, and especially since the coming of the railways, London's influence has spread far out. To-day the seaside towns conform to no common pattern, but present a rich diversity. There is Brighton, the seaside metropolis; Eastbourne, still urbane in a not-so-gentle world; Hastings, with its juxtaposition of almost self-conscious modernity and leisurely antiquity; Rye and Winchelsea, New Romney and Lydd that even the Second World War could not for long disturb in their peaceful charm; Hythe, as friendly, and Folkestone, as handsome a watering-place as England can show; Dover, the epitome of England's history, war-scarred, workaday, a little grimly aware that it is not as other towns; Deal and Walmer, pleasant resorts facing the great sea-lanes of the English Channel; Sandwich, where it seems always afternoon; Ramsgate, with its exquisite harbour and two dog-racing tracks; Broadstairs, Dickensian and neat; and Margate, with its miles of smooth sands that for two months in the year support an incredible number of human bodies.

The scene would have looked very different if we could have surveyed it in Henry VIII's reign. Brighton, Eastbourne, Folkestone, Ramsgate and Margate would have appeared as villages of little note, but we should have found that Hastings, New Romney, Hythe, Dover, Sandwich, Rye and Winchelsea were towns still of some importance, and almost touchily conscious of their still greater importance in earlier English history. For these towns constituted the unique confederation of the Cinque Ports and Two Ancient Towns. Besides these, the head ports, were a number of " limbs " or members loosely associated with them, some being mere villages and others towns which had received a royal grant of incorporation. The full list of members differed a little from time to time: as in Charles II's charter of 1668 to the Cinque Ports it is given on page 18. All of the members, except Brightlingsea in Essex, are in Kent or Sussex, and most of them are on the Channel coast, although Grange (part of Gillingham) is at the mouth of the Medway, and others, such as Bekesbourne, Fordwich, Sarre, West Hythe,

	Head Port	Corporate Members	Non-corporate Members
The Cinque Ports	Hastings .	Pevensey, Seaford .	Bulverhythe, Petit Iham, Hidney, Beakesbourne, and Grange, alias Grenche.
	New Romney	Lydd . . .	Broomhill, Old Romney, Dengemarsh, and Oswardstone.
	Hythe . .	. . . .	West Hythe.
	Dover . .	Folkestone, Faversham	Margate, St. John's, Goresend, Birchington Wood, alias Woodchurch, St. Peter's, Kingsdown, and Ringwould.
	Sandwich .	Fordwich . .	Deal, Walmer, Ramsgate, Stonar, Sarre, and Brightlingsea.
Two Ancient Towns	Rye . .	Tenterden . .	—
	Winchelsea .	—	—

Old Romney and Tenterden, as a result of coastal and river changes, have long since ceased to have any maritime connection.

Although this is not a work of history, it would be unthinkable to attempt any account of the Cinque Ports except against an historical background, for the traveller or sojourner in Dover or Rye, New Romney or Sandwich, Winchelsea or Hythe, quickly recognises there especially that the past is no less real and significant than the objects which his senses assure him are material and present. Few places more sharply evoke " a sense of the past "—a phrase which we may fairly borrow, for Henry James lived much at Rye in his later years. In this first chapter we shall therefore give some brief account of the way in which the Cinque Ports came into being, flourished for a while, reaching their zenith in the early fourteenth century, and then declined. This chapter deals for the most part with things that happened before 1600; in the remaining chapters, casting our net wider to include other and more recent events not necessarily related to the Confederation as such, we give a topographical note upon each of the Ports in turn.

The two most noteworthy features of the Cinque Ports are that, together, they formed a confederation which was without parallel amongst English constitutional institutions, and that, up to about the end of the thirteenth century, they provided the King's Navy, in so far as one could be said then to exist. That it should be the flourishing towns of the Kent and Sussex coast, with their profitable fishing trade, that were called upon for " ship service " was natural enough, for whether the King required ships for peaceful passage to the continent, or for fighting his wars, the English Channel was likely to be the *mise-en-scène.*

Whether the Confederation of the Cinque Ports existed before the Norman Conquest is uncertain; if it existed at all it was probably in informal fashion. But it is certain that ship-service preceded the Conquest, for Domesday Book records of Dover that in the time of Edward the Confessor the burgesses were liable to supply " to the King, once in the year, twenty ships for fifteen days, and in each ship were twenty-one men. This service they did because he had remitted to them the sac and soc " (*i.e.*, the right to hold a court, and to the profits arising from the jurisdiction). There was no need to specify whether the ships were to be men-of-war or transports, for in the eleventh century—and indeed for several centuries—they could be used indifferently for either purpose. The Bayeux Tapestry contains a lively contemporary illustration of what the Dover ships must have looked like; the official seals of the Ports, which show ships of a rather later date (p. 123), emphasise the strongly conservative fashion in boat design at this period.

Like Dover, the ports of Sandwich and Romney owed ship-service in return for sac and soc, and probably if the evidence were more complete we should find that the men of Hastings and Hythe also had entered into similar bargains with Edward the Confessor or his predecessors.

Duty for fifteen days in the year, and crews of twenty-one men (including a boy called a " grummet ") remained the units of the Cinque Ports ship-service even 300 years later, when ships were larger and campaigns more prolonged than in Edward the Confessor's day. At first glance fifteen days seems too brief a period for ship-service ever to have been of much practical value. But originally the ships were required either for peaceful passage to the continent, or to repel the sudden raids of the Norsemen, and the shortness of the period of service is therefore understandable.

William the Conqueror had ample reason to seek the good-will of the Ports. They commanded his lines of communication, and of possible retreat; they could, at will, protect his rear or leave it open to attack. In the next century we find Dover, Sandwich and Romney continued in their privileged positions, in which they were joined by Hastings and Hythe. In 1155 and 1156, Henry II granted charters to the Ports individually, confirming them in their privileges, which, in the main, were similar to those secured for themselves by other boroughs up and down the country. The portsmen were to be free of "lastage, tallage, passage, kayage, rivage, ponsage, and wreck" and other tolls and customs: they were to be "lovecope-free," i.e., free to trade, unhindered by any monopoly or merchant guild; they were to have their own courts and they could not be called upon to appear in the shire and the hundred courts. Many other boroughs enjoyed similar privileges, but two were peculiar to the Cinque Ports—"honours at court" and "den and strond."

Honours at court, the right of the portsmen, at every coronation, to carry the canopy over the King and his Queen (2), and afterwards to dine at the table nearest to the King's right hand, is dealt with in Chapter II. The privilege still exists in a modified form, and the Ports' representatives who take part in the ceremony bear, amongst the portsmen, the honourable title of "coronation barons." (The term "baron" originally meant merely a feudal tenant, and although later its use was generally restricted to the King's great tenants-in-chief, the predecessors of our House of Lords, nevertheless the men of the Cinque Ports continued to call themselves by that name). Nowadays the coronation barons, at the ceremony and on other subsequent solemn occasions, wear an elegant variant of eighteenth century court dress. The Cinque Ports have always had a proper understanding of the place and significance of pageantry and colour, even amidst the drabness of the twentieth century, as anyone who has had the good fortune to witness a Cinque Ports ceremony will gratefully acknowledge.

But to return to the Ports' privileges: " den and strond " was the right—and a valuable one, when fish formed a much larger part of the national diet than it now does—for the portsmen to land on the shore at Great Yarmouth, and to dry their nets and to dispose of their catch there. During the great herring fair at Yarmouth the Cinque Ports appointed bailiffs to ensure the keeping of the peace, a privilege which the men of Yarmouth came to resent more and more as a derogation from their own natural rights. On one occasion at least, a Cinque Ports bailiff was killed by a Yarmouth bailiff, a crime which the town was required to expiate by the payment of an annual tribute of herrings to St. George's Chapel, Windsor. The animosity between the men of Yarmouth and the portsmen reached a head in 1297, when the King's fleet, on its way to Sluys, was suddenly rent by an internecine squabble, the Cinque Ports contingent falling upon the Yarmouth ships, destroying thirty-two of them and killing over 200 men. Later the Admiral was warned to be more cautious and to keep the Yarmouth and Cinque Ports ships safely apart, but the royal displeasure made little difference to the habits of the portsmen. They must have been a turbulent and troublesome crew.

The Cinque Ports had so many interests and activities in common—ship-service, den and strond, honours at court, exemptions from tolls and customs, and from suit at the shire and hundred courts, not to mention private quarrels with Yarmouth and other ports, English and foreign—that it was natural for them to evolve common institutions. By the middle of the twelfth century the Court of Shepway had come into existence. It was for the Cinque Ports what the shire court was for the county, and it took its name from the lathe (as the major territorial divisions in Kent are called) in which it was held. According to tradition, the meeting-place of the Court was first of all at Lympne; whether the Court did in fact meet there or not, if you take the trouble to visit the stone cross, erected in 1923 by the seventh Lord Beauchamp, Lord Warden and Admiral, at the top of Lympne Hill to mark the Court's supposed meeting-place and to commemorate the historic deeds of the Ports, you will be well rewarded for your pains by the panorama of Romney Marsh which stretches away southward, with the sea beyond. Here you stand on the top of the ancient coastal cliff, and below lies the level of the Marsh, where 2,000 years ago the sea rolled and the Roman galleys plied their trade between Britain and Gaul. Above all in the evening, when the sheep on the rich pastures far below acquire solid, stilted shadows and the discordance of Dymchurch's bungalows and holiday-camps is muted by the distance and by the all-embracing harmony of the sunset, the scene, so different now from what once it was, induces a strange nostalgia—more than the nostalgia of an individual or of a generation: perhaps it is not too fanciful to describe it as a folk-nostalgia. Here, as so often in the Cinque Ports country, only a little sympathy and a little imagination are wanted for the past to come alive.

The Court of Shepway was presided over by a royal officer, the Warden of the Cinque Ports, just as the shire court was presided over by the King's sheriff. Wardens first appear in the thirteenth century, and from the time of Edward I the office has been combined with the Constableship of Dover Castle. Although it was a royal appointment, the Warden at his installation took an oath—as he still does—to uphold the liberties and privileges of the Cinque Ports. The Court of Shepway, as recently as 1946, met in order that the Right Honourable Winston Churchill, C.H., might take his oath when he became Lord Warden (3), a fit successor to an office once held by Admiral Blake, William Pitt, and Wellington, amongst other notable defenders of the realm. The Constable and Warden had several courts, some in his capacity as Constable of the Castle, others as Warden of the Ports, but the theoretical distinctness of the courts does not seem to have been preserved in practice. At first the courts were held in the Castle, but as the Castle itself was extra-territorial to the Cinque Ports, it was in the " foreign " to the portsmen, and by royal grant they were not to be impleaded in the " foreign." To overcome this difficulty, the meeting-place of the courts was early transferred to old St. James's Church, which stood below the Castle wall, and was thus within the liberties of the Cinque Ports. St. James's, a Norman church, was badly damaged during the Second World War; in 1950, suddenly, its half-destroyed tower crashed down, and much of what was left of the ruins had to be removed for safety's sake.

The Warden also enjoyed the office of Admiral of the Cinque Ports, and as such had jurisdiction from Redcliff, near Seaford in Sussex, to Shoe Beacon in Essex " half-sea over," *i.e.*, to mid-Channel. In his Court of Admiralty he enquired into wrecks, prizes taken at sea, and allegations of piracy. Wrecks gave rise to many legal conundrums, complicated by the fact that the Crown, the Warden, and the Cinque Ports were all entitled to a share of the spoils. From complaints made in the Admiralty Court it is only too plain that the portsmen sometimes forgot the charter of 1236, which declared that if a man or beast escaped alive from a stranded vessel it was not a wreck, open to the depredations of the first finder; and it was even alleged— apparently with some reason—that they were not above plying the pirates' trade under colour of salvaging a wreck.

In spite of his oath to defend the liberties of the Cinque Ports, the Lord Warden sometimes proved, for the Courts, an uncomfortable and over-powerful ally. His courts drew away profitable business from their courts, and they were impotent to prevent this filching of their jurisdiction. His aid might be useful on occasion, but it was to be had at a price, as Faversham had discovered long before; in 1305 the town made the Warden a gift of " 100 salt fish, called grayling," to have his favour in a dispute between the burgesses and their overlord, the Abbot of Faversham, and more than eighty years later his successor was still claiming, as of right, an annual oblation of fish from the men of Faversham. An inquest summoned at Chilham in 1388 found that the Warden was not entitled to his grayling. Well might Jeake, the first historian of the Cinque Ports, writing in 1678, exclaim that the Wardens had usurped upon the Ports' privileges " as, if it were more convenient, I could sufficiently demonstrate." Perhaps the high-water (or should it be low-water?) mark of the Warden's avarice was the charging of groundage to a vessel that had run on to the Goodwins, but was lucky enough to get off again—in compensation for the damage done by the ship to his sands!

Two other courts, or assemblies, grew up to deal with the affairs of the Cinque Ports—the Brodhull (now called the Brotherhood) and the Guestling. The Brodhull was meeting as early as the thirteenth century at a place called "Broadhill," which is now lost. Afterwards it was transferred to New Romney, and, the significance of the earlier name having been forgotten, in the fifteenth century it became known as the "Brotherhood." Usually it met twice a year, its main function being to ensure that the Ports' privileges at Yarmouth were properly respected at each year's herring-fair. In New Romney Town Hall are two books, the White Book and the Black Book of the Cinque Ports, which contain an unbroken record of the meeting of the Brotherhood from 1433 to the present day.

The Guestling began, in the fourteenth century, as an assembly, no doubt at first rather informal, of the three western ports of Hastings, Winchelsea and Rye, meeting probably at the village of Guestling, near Winchelsea. The convenience of neighbouring ports holding meetings in this way was so apparent that the practice was copied by the Kent ports, and after 1481 they are to be found convening their own "Guestlings" after the manner of their Sussex confederates. During the next century Guestlings began to be held for all the Ports. A Guestling differed from a Brotherhood in that it did not always meet at the same town, and that it included representatives not only of the Head Ports, but also of the corporate members—whence earlier etymologists deduced that as the members came as guests the court acquired its name of Guestling; it is a pity that most of the more enterprising etymological guesses prove to be wrong. During the declining years of the Cinque Ports, as the business fell away both in volume and in weight, the Brotherhood and the Guestling were combined. Occasionally, with archaic and ceremonious formality, meetings are still "arreared" when matters of importance to the Cinque Ports need to be discussed, matters, for instance, such as the due recognition of the Ports' "honours at court" at a coronation.

In addition to this constitutional machinery evolved by the

Confederation, each town had its own court and assembly, and its own legal customs recorded in the town's custumal. So elaborate a constitutional organisation is evidence of the importance to which the Cinque Ports attained in the centuries following the Norman Conquest. From 1066 until 1204, when King John lost Normandy, there was little naval activity, but with the loss of Normandy the English Channel, and with it the Cinque Ports, take on a new significance. The portsmen seem already to have acquired for themselves a reputation for diligence in promoting their own interests without too nice a regard for the rights of others (some did not scruple to denominate their activities piracy), and King John, doubtless hoping to gain their support, granted the Ports a series of charters in 1205. But it was probably less from a sense of gratitude than from a lively expectation of favours to come that the Cinque Ports fleet, in the battle which took place off Sandwich in 1217, routed the much larger fleet bringing reinforcements to Louis, French claimant to the English crown, and so ensured that the Plantagenets should remain on the throne. In this battle the portsmen adopted the ruse, no doubt regarded at the time as unchivalrous, of blinding their foes by throwing quick-lime over their ships.

In the Barons' War, the Cinque Ports were courted by both parties; giving unwavering allegiance to neither, they lent their aid, on the whole, to Simon de Montfort. His success was short-lived; Prince Edward defeated him at Evesham, and proceeded to deal with a number of over-zealous adherents to the de Montfort cause. Winchelsea was among the offenders, and Edward severely reprimanded the townsmen, telling them " not henceforth to apply themselves to plunder like pirates." Whenever the portsmen were admonished they had a ready answer, that they would " forthwith forsake their wives and children, and all that they had, and go to make their profit on the sea, wheresoever they thought that they would be able to acquire it." The fact that such a threat could be made, and that it was no empty one, shows how slackly the reins of government were held by the King. Indeed, at this time the Ports enjoyed something approaching semi-independence. Their predatory

c

exploits were notorious. In 1242 the portsmen received royal
authority to ravage the French coast, sparing only the churches
and accounting to the King for one-fifth of the plunder; with
their usual fine disregard for narrow considerations of nationality
they robbed and killed French and English merchants alike.
A few years earlier a Spanish vessel lying in Sandwich haven
had been boarded, her crew killed, and her cargo stolen.
Throughout the thirteenth and fourteenth centuries complaints
against the piratical practices of the portsmen were frequent.
In 1314, for example, the men of Winchelsea were authorised
to equip two ships to protect the coast against pirates; but
long-standing habits are not so easily cast off, and within a
month one of the two had committed at least half a dozen acts
of piracy. Some twenty years later the barons of the same port
had the audacity to plunder one of the King's own ships whilst
it was lying at anchor there. At this time the portsmen were
very much a law (or an unlaw) unto themselves, and although
with varying degrees of assiduity Henry III and the first three
Edwards all tried to persuade the portsmen into more obedient
and more orthodox behaviour, they could scarcely be satisfied
with their success—especially as, repeatedly, they had to pay
compensation from the royal treasury to foreign ports and
merchants for losses suffered at the hands of the portsmen.

Not content with demonstrating, through these piratical
exploits, their partial immunity from the King's power, the
portsmen carried on what amounted to private wars with other
ports, English and foreign. In 1292, the Cinque Ports, with
their Dutch, Irish and Gascon allies, defeated a combined
Norman, French and Genoese fleet in a pitched battle fought
at a pre-arranged spot in the Channel. They carried on an
intermittent warfare with the Bayonnais, and during the first
half of the fourteenth century maintained a standing feud with
Fowey and other west country ports.

The end of the thirteenth and the beginning of the fourteenth
century saw the Cinque Ports at the zenith of their power.
Winchelsea and Rye now became full and independent members
of the Confederation, under the style of the Two Ancient
Towns, instead of being mere appendages of Hastings. The

association of other Kent and Sussex towns and villages with the Cinque Ports as " limbs " or " members " (the terms are interchangeable) which has already been mentioned seems to have come about casually and with an absence of official direction typical of our earlier constitutional processes; apparently there was not even an authoritative list of the Cinque Ports and their members until 1293, when Stephen de Pencestre, as Warden, made a return of them to the Exchequer. The members shared with their Head Port the burden of ship-service, and their own town or village government was subject to some degree of supervision by the Head Port; in return they enjoyed some of the privileges of the Cinque Ports, and, perhaps even more important, could invoke the powerful aid of the Confederation in dealings with their seigniorial overlord. Several of the members, notably Folkestone, Margate, Ramsgate and Deal, eventually surpassed their Head Ports in size. Some of the more important members secured royal charters confirming their position in the Confederation, but the arrangements with the smaller, unincorporate, members were never regarded as requiring royal sanction.

However, by the fourteenth century conditions were changing. Little ships, manned by a crew of twenty-one (even including a " grummet ") were of small value in naval warfare after it had passed beyond the stage of guerilla tactics, and it is significant that in 1306 the Ports' assessment was reduced from fifty-seven to twenty-seven ships, although the total complement of men was to remain the same as before. Moreover, spells of fifteen days were not long enough now to be of much use, and it became customary for the portsmen to serve beyond the fifteen days on payment of 6d. a day to the master of the vessel, the same to the constable, and 3d. a day each to the rest of the crew. The failing fortunes of the Ports were emphasised by the fact that Edward III, as " an especial grace," bore half of the cost of the twenty-one ships that they furnished in 1340 for the Battle of Sluys. The Ports, too, having for long sown the wind, now began to reap the whirlwind. French raids on the English coast became more frequent and more vigorous, Rye and Winchelsea especially being singled out for attack. As for Hythe, the burgesses were in such a plight, as the result of raids, fire and pestilence, that they would have abandoned the town if Henry IV had not persuaded them to remain by promising to remit their service for a time. Without much success the ports tried to protect themselves by throwing up defence works. It is to this period that the earthen ramparts at Sandwich, the town wall at Dover, and the gateways at Rye, belong. In the 1380's both Rye and Sandwich petitioned for aid in walling their towns, being now too poor to bear the charge themselves.

The decline in the importance of the Cinque Ports was shown, too, by the fact that never again after 1414 were they called upon to perform their ship-service in full. During Henry VIII's reign they did modified ship-service three times; in 1588 their contribution to the fleet that was England's defence against the Armada consisted of the *Elisabeth* or *Elnathan* (120 tons) of Dover, the *Reuben* (110 tons) of Sandwich, the *William* (80 tons) of Rye, the *Ann Bonaventure* (70 tons) of Hastings, the *John* (60 tons) of Romney, the *Grace of God* (50 tons) of Hythe, and the *Hazard* (38 tons) of Faversham—a small enough contingent for so serious an occasion. Incidentally, Dover was still, at this time, of sufficient importance to house a Spanish spy.

After the end of the sixteenth century, whenever the Cinque Ports provided vessels for the royal use they did so upon payment, in the same way as other coastal and riverside towns. The growing disparity between their privileges and their duties did not appeal to the frugal Elizabeth, who announced in 1587 that "she doth not meane to suffer them in suche fruiteless manner to enjoye so great privileges without doing any service, but to resume them into Her Majesty's hands and to reduce them to the same terms that the rest of her subjects bordering upon the sea coasts are in." But even Elizabeth found this either impossible or inexpedient. Indeed, as the Cinque Ports' privileges became less and less defensible with the passage of time, so the portsmen exerted more and more effort—successfully, on the whole—in defending them.

What were the causes of this collapse in the fortunes of the

Ports, after the devil-may-care days of freebooting and independence at the turn of the thirteenth century ? One cause, perhaps the most important and certainly the most startling, beyond the wit of man to counter, was the way in which the Kent and Sussex coastline changed, especially in the fifteenth century. At Hastings the sea gained upon the land, but elsewhere, for example, at New Romney, Rye, Hythe and Sandwich, the sea was retreating before sand-banks and shingle-banks, the harbours were silting up, and the ports were being left stranded, far from the sea. In 1586 Camden says of Sandwich " the harbour by the sand driven in and a great merchant ship of Pope Paul IV (sic) sunk in the very middle of it, is not capable of admitting large ships." By constant exertion and with royal support Dover managed, but only just, to keep its harbour open. Hythe and New Romney, of less strategic importance, could not look for the same assistance; they retired from the struggle and from the sea. When, in 1637, Charles I made his third demand for ship-money, the Cinque Ports begged some remission, saying that there was not a single fishing-boat at New Romney or Lydd, and only a few at Hythe, beached a mile from the town. Rye made repeated and valiant attempts to preserve its harbour, and in 1722 we find the Ryers writing to other seaports in the country, begging their good offices in securing yet another Act of Parliament for the benefit of the harbour because if " some speedy Care be not taken it will be totally Lost to the great prejudice of Trade . . . ye said Port is so situate that from Dover to Portsmouth there is not any Harbour to Receive Shipping in Distress or give them Shelter in time of War from Ships of the Enemy." At New Romney even as recently as the middle of the last century it was possible to take a small boat up the creek to St. Nicholas' Church, but the inning of the area that is now the suburb of Littlestone deprived New Romney town of its last physical connection with the sea. To discuss, at length, the causes of the coastal changes would be out of place here, and besides even experts do not find these waters plain sailing. It must suffice to notice that these physiographical changes occurred, and that only at Dover were human efforts of some avail to withstand their disastrous effects.

It is tempting to suppose that, if Nature had not played this out-of-the-way trick, the Cinque Ports would all still be busy commercial ports. But coastal changes were not the only reason for the decline in their fortunes, a decline which had indeed begun to appear in the fourteenth century, a hundred years or more before the topographical changes became most serious. The real causes of the decline were present from the beginning. The ascendancy of the Ports was largely due to the combination of a favourable geographical position and the political accidents of the thirteenth century. It was a fictitious prosperity, lacking any sound economic basis. Fishing, even if eked out with a little piracy and wrecking, placed the Cinque Ports in no position to compete with other ports, such as Southampton and London, mostly of somewhat later development, whose prosperity rested on the more solid foundations of commerce. Even at Sandwich, with its prosperous hinterland, where trade was fairly extensive up to the sixteenth century, it was mainly in the hands of foreigners. In 1619 the Cinque Ports had to report to the Lord Warden that there was only one ship, a 50-ton vessel plying to Malaga and Bordeaux, which traded overseas; all the rest traded coast-wise only, to other parts of England, although some few passage-boats made the crossing to France, Holland and Flanders. They add, significantly, that many owners and masters of larger ships had removed themselves to the port of London.

Thus it was a lucky combination of circumstances that promoted the fortunes of the Ports, and a series of unlucky coincidences that first caused their decline and then prevented their revival. By the time of Queen Elizabeth the Cinque Ports had ceased to be of any special significance in England's development; but for the historian, and for the topographer with an affection for the ghosts of the past who refuse to be still, the Cinque Ports can never be insignificant.

CHAPTER II

HASTINGS

HASTINGS is now by common consent accepted as the premier of the Cinque Ports. The grounds of its claim to this position we shall first review, and we shall then be in a position to consider the history of the Port and to understand the seeming incongruity by which the chief business of the Ports was transacted not at Hastings but at Dover.

Although not mentioned in Domesday Book, Hastings must by then already have become an important place. In 928 it was of sufficient standing to be included in the Laws of Athelstan as a place possessing a mint, and in 1052 Godwin was able, in the words of the Saxon Chronicle, to ". . . entice to him all the Kentish men, and all the boatmen from Hastings and everywhere thereabout by the sea-coast. . . ."

Hastings' premiership used to be thought a mark of approval granted to his favourite port by the Conqueror, with the result that it was usually named first in the general charters granted to the Ports. William, it is well known, made quickly for Hastings after his landing at Pevensey a short distance westward (to obtain food, according to the inscription on the Bayeux Tapestry), and it may well be that his choice of Hastings as a base was governed by that town's continued friendly relation with the Abbey of Fécamp to which, with other property in the large manor of Rameslie, it had been first granted by Canute. Hastings, in fact, may have served as the port of the manor. However, another explanation is that Hastings was named first merely in relation to its prior place in the recitation of the Ports from west to east, this being the generally accepted geographical order. Yet another explanation was that the barons of Hastings alone among the Ports were owners of land at the herring-fishery fair of Yarmouth in the middle years of the twelfth century. There is certainly evidence that several of the Ports took part in the Yarmouth herring-fishery and its accompanying fair in times before the Conquest. In any event, this claim to the premiership, which was bound up to a large extent with the Coronation privileges, was not made by Hastings before 1369. In the portsmen's own courts the question of precedence also gave rise to much contention, until at last the relative seniority was settled at the Brotherhood held in 1615 and Hastings was recognised in its premiership.

The claim has not since been challenged. Hastings heads the list of the Ports; in the Courts of Brotherhood and Guestling it occupies the seat of honour on the Speaker's right hand, except when it is itself Speaker in rotation, while at the Lord Warden's Court of Shepway it takes a similar place. But for matters of administration, Dover has long since been regarded as the chief Port, mainly because there the foremost officer of the Confederation, the Lord Warden, who was also Constable of the Royal Castle, had his headquarters.

The story of the port of Hastings is an instructive study in historical geography. In absolute chronology it occupies ten centuries, and its active life a very great deal less, but it is set against a much wider background, a relative time-scale for which is provided by the form and nature of a constantly changing coast-line. In brief, the maritime history of Hastings is to be traced in the irregular but progressive erosion of its seaboard, and in the slow accumulation of an extensive fringe of flint-pebble shingle.

At the time when the Haestingas, the tribe whose name is perpetuated in the place-name, were settled in this district two streams here met the sea, and at the mouth of one of them, Priory Stream, and in the lee of White Rock stood the Saxon harbour. This harbour was probably the successor to an even earlier one sited at Bulverhythe to the west. The gradual breaking down of the protective sandstone and clay cliffs and the erosion of White Rock subjected it to the full force of the powerful eastward longshore drift; the low coastline foundered, the Priory stream commenced to silt, and the harbour was drowned. A new town, the "New Burgh" of Domesday Book, grew up in the valley between West Hill, crowned by the castle of William I, and East Hill; a small stream called the Bourne ran down through the valley, and at its mouth on the

6 THE BEACHED FISHING FLEET

7 NET-HOUSES ON THE STADE

HASTINGS

8   PELHAM CRESCENT : a Regency sea-front (1823)

HASTINGS

seashore was a harbour. The harbour was a shallow anchorage at the best of times, and with falls of cliff which diminished the flow of the Bourne and the growth of a shingle bar it presently became useless to shipping. In the middle of the sixteenth century the condition of the harbour was causing anxiety; by the end of the century it was no longer of major account. The portsmen tried at various times to secure the advantages of a pier-anchorage, but always the prevailing up-channel winds and the shingle drift have proved its ruin. The tumbled masonry of the last attempt made in 1893 can still be seen near the present Fishmarket. The site of the old harbour is now a rising shingle bank, and a fun fair and an artificial lake for miniature boats occupy the place of the one-time berths of the Cinque Ports ships.

The town was in its heyday at the end of the eleventh century and the beginning of the twelfth. It then controlled a much-used passage to France, and although the Conqueror had kept his vow to return to Fécamp the lands held by them in the days of Edward the Confessor, and thus much of the land about Hastings, he retained control of the " New Burgh " and its guardian castle on the hill above. By the end of the twelfth century the harbour was proving unserviceable owing to the inundations of the sea. Winchelsea and Rye were in the ascendancy, the barons of Hastings complaining bitterly that the growing wealth of their neighbours was detrimental to the Head Port. At the same time, the castle was falling into ruin, and in 1339 and 1377 the town and its ships were sacked by the French. By the middle of the sixteenth century it was described as being reduced to " waste, destruction and poverty."

Hastings had sunk to the relative obscurity of a fishing village, although important enough, in the seventeenth century, to send its fish regularly by pack-horse to London. From this state it rose only towards the end of the eighteenth century when sea-bathing became fashionable. The early years of its new prosperity are marked by the sea-front expansion of pleasant bow-windowed terrace houses with their light iron balconies, the villas of Breed's Place and the adjoining Pelham Cres-cent (8, 15), with the cliff cut away to accommodate the early nineteenth century neo-classical church of St. Mary-in-the-Castle. The well-mannered cream and golden-hued stucco of the sea-front is now unhappily disappearing: a rough-cast finish gives better protection against winter gales, but at the cost of this mellow tradition.

The shipmen of Hastings were well known in the outside world. Perhaps their outstanding service beyond Britain was that in the crusading expedition of 1148 when Lisbon was taken from the Moors and settled again on Alfonso, King of Portugal; in this curious way a priest of Hastings became a bishop of Lisbon. It is not possible to speak of all the official engagements into which they entered. Two ships accompanied Edward I to Scotland in 1300; five ships and ninety-six men took part in the siege of Calais in 1347; and two centuries later, in the fleet against the Armada, Hastings men were still to be found in action. Of their unofficial engagements there is good evidence in the repeated complaints from merchants of Cologne, Bruges, Ypres and many other places who had lost their cargoes upon the high seas. These activities, and the familiarity of the Hastings fishermen with the inshore channels (there were thirty-three boats of some 30 tons in 1641), provided the experience to be inherited by the contraband runners of the eighteenth century, of which the port had a notorious number.

The harbour has gone, but Hastings fishermen are still to be found upon The Stade, where the picturesque net-houses (7), the tall gaunt huts of tarred wood in which their gear is dried, are a distinctive feature of the shore. Set against the ochre background of the East Hill cliffs and with the fishing fleet drawn high up by capstans on the shingle nearby (6), they have caught the eye of many an artist. Among the famous were Turner, Peter de Wint and David Cox, but others much less well known have painted here with delight and satisfaction, as may be seen in the small but enjoyable collection of topographical pictures in the Old Town Hall.

There is now, it is said, a proposal to pull down some of the more decayed houses and to replace them with modern net-shops, but most of us would look askance at such an end to a pleasant and favourite tourist-trophy. Next to go would be the few remaining weather-boarded houses, now chiefly tea-shops, the white and green jellied eel stalls, the cockle men, and all the tawdry romance which makes this free-and-easy fishing quarter such an apposite relief to the shabby gentility of much of suburban Hastings.

Landward of The Stade, the valley between the two great hills is still occupied by the " New Burgh," which in the process of time has come to be called the Old Town. This is the Hastings of historic interest, a sea-side town overlooked by its medieval castle on the brow of the western hill. Two narrow streets, High Street and All Saints' Street, occupy most of the floor of the valley and indeed cut into its sides if we may judge by the foot-walks raised up above the level of the roads themselves. The tightly packed red tile roofs, with an occasional chimney stack of thin red brick to give a clue to their age, cover houses in a charming variety. There are the bad gaps of war-damage still to be seen, but the seventeenth century timber-framed and plastered houses which escaped are not hard to find (24), and with the red and black brick of the early eighteenth century, and the tall bow-windows and imitation brick tile-hanging of the houses built towards the end of that period, they make a picturesque show. At the very foot of the valley, and somewhere near the former mouth of the Bourne stream, in the backyard of a block of modern flats, are the last remaining pieces of the Town Wall, a wall of flint and sandstone built in the fourteenth century as a defence against the town's chief enemies, the French and the sea. There is another piece close by behind the Royal Standard Inn, a poor relic of a wall which once had three gates and a tower at each end. In the sixteenth and seventeenth centuries, a gun-garden under the wall was furnished with guns in anticipation of attacks by the French.

Close by is the Old Town Hall, the lower part of which is a museum. Its noteworthy collection of coronation relics is sufficient excuse for the next two or three paragraphs about honours at court, mentioned briefly in Chapter I.

The barons claimed by inherent custom and prescription the right to support over the heads of the King and Queen, upon four silver staves, a square canopy of cloth of gold or purple silk having at each corner a small gilded silver bell (2), and to dine, on the day of the coronation, at a table on the King's right hand. Each canopy was to be carried by sixteen barons, four at each corner. The canopy, staves and bells were the fee for their services, though from time to time they preferred a claim, which was usually disallowed, for cloth for their vestments at the cost of the King. At one time the barons of Hastings were wont to present their canopy to the Shrine of St. Richard at Chichester, while the men of the eastern ports offered theirs to St. Thomas at Canterbury.

There was sometimes difficulty in the choice of the coronation barons. James I insisted upon " men of the netest and comlyest personage amongest you." Mary D'Este of Modena, queen of James II, demanded men whom she knew personally. The barons' costume is of distinct sartorial interest. According to the custumals of Winchelsea and Rye, they were to appear " solemnly and decently clothed and apparelled with one suit of their own proper costs," but they have in fact worn various styles of uniform which have been promulgated from time to time at the Courts of Brotherhood. For example, at the coronation of James II in 1684 (2), the barons wore doublets of crimson satin, scarlet hose, scarlet gowns faced with crimson and caps and shoes of black velvet. The resplendent uniforms worn by Edward Milward and his son Edward, both barons of Hastings, at the coronations of George III and George IV, may at present be seen in the Museum at John's Place. Yet another uniform, of which there is an example in the Old Town Hall Museum, was designed for the coronation of Edward VII, and it is this which is worn by the barons of the present day.

There are other interesting relics in the museum cases: a piece of Queen Anne's canopy, red silk with yellow fringe, pieces of early Georgian cloth-of-gold, rich and heavy, patterned with birds and sprays of roses and with a 5-inch border of gold thread; part of a silver stave; and casts of bells. A silver punch bowl was made from the staves and bells of George II's canopy, and a chandelier for St. Clement's Church (it is the eastern one of the two in the nave) from the staves which held the canopy over George III in 1761 (10).

At the coronation of Charles II in 1660 there was a most unseemly brawl between the footmen of the royal household and the barons over the possession of the canopy, and much trouble over the barons' seats at the dinner table. Pepys, who was there, " observed little disorder in all this, only the King's footmen had got hold of the canopy," but his attention was no doubt being devoted to the " brave ladies " who filled the hall. At the coronation banquet of his successor in 1685 there were no less than 1,445 separate dishes—as many as 144 in a single dining mess—and there is little wonder that the barons were anxious to secure their proper seats at such a meal. The variety of fish alone included " lamprey, salmon, cold lobster, cold pickled oysters, anchoviz, cold souc'd carp, souc'd trouts, marmoted fish cold, crafish, periwinkles, cockles, mullet, prawns, crabs, and collar'd eeles."

The coronation of George IV was the last occasion on which the barons were allowed their full honours at court. It may have been hot weather for this " very laborious Service," but for one reason or another—their official report said it was " impossible to carry it steadily for want of a previous exercise, it was found awkward and difficult to manage "—the barons did not perform their canopy service again. The King no longer walks from his Palace to the Abbey, and the practical need for a canopy does not now exist. There is, however, a substituted service, which was instituted at the coronation of Edward VII: the barons now line the west side of the screen in the Abbey, " close to where they would have remained had Canopies been used," and receive for custody the standards borne before their Majesties. So continues, in a new form, an honour of which there is written record in 1189 at the coronation of Richard I.

Among the buildings of the Old Town are two medieval churches of note. St. Clement (9), chiefly of the thirteenth century, has Cinque Port connections in its handsome chandelier, already mentioned, and in the wall monument to Thomas Delves, a seventeenth century baron. Its remarkable Perpendicular font carved with the Instruments of the Passion is one of the finest of its period. All Saints', with its noble tower, is a Perpendicular church built to replace the fabric destroyed by the French, only small traces of which now remain. There was once a complete scheme of contemporary wall paintings, among which, in the Chapel of St. Nicholas, could be found pictures of ships and maritime scenes, but all save the lifeless Doom above the chancel arch have been " restored " away. Both churches possessed hangings made from coronation canopies, the gift of devout barons. The dedication of Basil Champney's Catholic church, St. Mary Star-of-the-Sea, in 1882 forged a notable modern link between church and sea.

This short topography of Hastings started with William the Conqueror; it must close with the Conqueror's Stone. It lies on Marina, in the flower bed opposite the entrance to the Palace Pier. It was either the Conqueror's dining-table or King Harold's grave-stone, and perhaps only Mr. James Burton, who laid out the seaside town of St. Leonards in 1828, and then discovered it, could tell us which.

Bulverhythe, a neighbouring place which was a non-corporate member of Hastings, has been partly engulfed by the sea. Its name denotes the landing-place or hythe of the people of the " burgh," that is, the port of the Hastings people, and it seems to be the earliest port of this ancient settlement. The Bulverhythe of to-day, the western seaside suburb of Hastings, stands on a reclaimed marsh, and the only reminders of the once flourishing port which has been washed away by the sea are the weather-boarded Bull Inn and the fragmentary remains of an early medieval chapel. This chapel, its site now carefully preserved among modern houses by the Corporation of Hastings, was once a prebend of St. Mary-in-the-Castle, but no records of it are known after the fourteenth century.

It is worth while trying to time a visit to Bulverhythe at an exceptionally low tide, for there are then visible off Galley Hill the tree-stumps of a submerged forest. Here, much more readily than in the text-books, does one understand the changes in the relative levels of land and sea in a remote (but geologically recent) time. There is scarcely a better piece of instructive geology anywhere in Sussex, but it is rarely to be seen. The curious may also hear at times, and with a west wind, the sound of Bulverhythe Bells, the harsh raking noise of the shingle beach which, by some trick of echo, has an unmistakable clangour of its own. It is said to be a sure forecast of a storm, as it certainly was on our last visit.

Somewhere in this neighbourhood was Storisdale, the stream in which the criminals of Hastings adjudged to death were executed by drowning, according to the code of the Hastings custumal. Each of the Ports had its own method, usually brutal, of disposing of its malefactors; honours at court and picturesque buildings represent only one side of medieval life.

THE ARMS OF THE CINQUE PORTS

CHAPTER III

DOVER

IT is impossible to remain neutral about Dover; either you dismiss it as a town of mouldering drabness, a necessary but regrettable stage in the journey to or from the Continent, or you succumb to its *je ne sais quoi* and become as jealous a zealot as any native Dovorian. We freely confess ourselves to be devotees, but whether we can communicate our fond enthusiasm to those who have not fallen under Dover's uncanny charm is problematical; the poets prudently advise the lover against analysing the reasons for his affections, and in any case a *je ne sais quoi* ought to defy description and analysis. But possibly where our words fail the photographs may succeed.

Whichever way you approach Dover, the Castle is paramount. The least impressive approach is along the road from Deal, for although the Castle can be seen squatly on the horizon, not until you get to the top of Castle Hill does its massiveness and its dominance over the town in the valley beneath become apparent (12). The traveller from Canterbury going slowly down the upper slope of the long hill into Lydden has a brief vignette of the five-mile distant Castle, but catches no glimpse of it again until he reaches Dover, to find it remote and aloof on its tree-covered hill, brooding over the town. The traveller from Folkestone, on the other hand, first sees the Castle when he is by the " Royal Oak," four miles out of Dover, and then has it in sight, framed by the V of the valley, for the rest of his journey. It is a view which is so susceptible to the weather as to give the illusion that the physical features themselves are as mutable as the clouds; on a day of drought and sun the Castle retires, insignificantly, almost out of the landscape, but on a sunless day, with scudding cloud and rain, its grey menacing bulk dominates the scene. But of all views of the Castle probably none is so impressive, or generally so welcome, as that which greets the returning continental voyager as his ship nears

10   A CHANDELIER, the gift of the Hastings barons who did canopy service at the coronation of George III in 1761, " Being the produce of their silver staves."

HASTINGS : ST. CLEMENT'S CHURCH

11 DOVER : The Gateway to England

the much publicised, yet still spectacular, White Cliffs of Dover (1, 11).

Since the Castle is Dover's cynosure, our note on the town may fittingly begin there. To do justice to it in a few pages is impossible; fortunately the Ministry of Works publish an excellent, and cheap, descriptive pamphlet. The greater part of the Castle is open freely to the public, but, as the notice board advises, admission to the Keep costs 1s. (although if you are a child or a " genuine party of 20 or more " the charge is halved) and the Underground Works are 2d. each. You are unlikely, anywhere, to get a richer return for your money, for Dover is a veritable museum of castle-building, with contributions from all periods, beginning with King Harold and ending with the 1939–45 war.

There are two entrances to the Castle, the lower, and nearer to the town (and therefore the more convenient for most pedestrians) being by way of the Canons' Gate, the upper, with the nearby car-park, through Constable's Gate. The Canons' Gate is a late eighteenth century insertion in the thirteenth century outer curtain wall. The Constable's Gate (17) was built during Henry III's reign, but has been a good deal modified to make it more commodious and convenient to the generations of Deputy Governors and Commanding Officers who have successively inhabited it. The windows and the stone balcony over the entrance gateway no doubt have added to commodiousness and convenience and are so incongruous as to be beyond offence.

The earliest building to be erected on Castle Hill—indeed, perhaps the oldest extant building in the country—was the pharos or lighthouse, put up by the Romans, probably before the year A.D. 100. The pharos stands at the west end of the Church of St. Mary-within-the-Castle (14), itself of late Saxon construction ; but old as the church is, the pharos stood on the hill in its pristine loneliness, for even longer than it has shared the hill with church and castle—a useful reminder that, contrary to the impression left by the history books, William the Conqueror was separated from Julius Cæsar by a longer interval of time than that which separates us from the Norman Conquest.

The pharos now stands about 40 feet high, but probably originally reached twice that height, with a beacon on the top. The lower four stages of the tower are Roman, but the fifth, and topmost extant stage, is of medieval construction. The original Roman tower was square internally, and octagonal externally, each stage being set back about a foot, so that the building had a stepped exterior, like a Dutch gable. Time, and stone-hungry medieval builders, have deprived the pharos of its original neat silhouette. The Castle pharos had its twin on the Western Heights, where the remains of a second Roman light-house were thus described by Camden in 1586: " On the other opposite rock which is almost level on the top are the remains of a very ancient building. Somebody, on what authority I know not, has called it Cæsar's Altar; but John Twine of Canterbury, a learned old man, who in his youth had seen it almost entire, assured me it was a Pharos to direct ships by fire in the night." These ruined foundations, surmounted by a lump of masonry known as the Bredenstone (5), were the site where, for some centuries, new Lord Wardens were wont to be sworn in, but the Bredenstone became overlaid by nineteenth century defence works, so that to-day its truncated and displaced remnants are to be seen only on application to the barracks guard. In the museum at the Maison Dieu can be seen Roman tiles taken out from these foundations, and stamped CL BR, *Classis Britannica*, the " British Fleet," which, even as early as the first century A.D., maintained a Channel patrol. Also on the Western Heights, not far from the Bredenstone, stand the foundations of a round-naved church, built about 1150, which was claimed in 1340 by the Prior of the Hospital of St. John of Jerusalem in England under the name of the " Chapel of Braddone." Possibly it was here (though perhaps more likely at Temple Ewell) that King John of England, in 1213, surrendered his kingdom to Pandulph, to receive it back at a papal fief.

But an even more interesting church than the Chapel of Braddone is St. Mary-within-the-Castle (14), which stands against the pharos on the Castle Hill—indeed, for centuries the pharos was physically joined to the church and served as a

12   THE CASTLE FROM THE AIR

13   THE SEA-FRONT AT WATERLOO CRESCENT

DOVER

14   THE EARLY ELEVENTH CENTURY CHURCH OF ST. MARY-IN-THE-CASTLE, with the adjacent Roman lighthouse

west tower. In plan the church is cruciform, with a central tower more to be admired for its massiveness and impression of strength than for its elegance. It used to be thought that the building was of Roman origin, but in fact the church was built shortly before the Norman Conquest, probably in the reign of Canute. The large quantity of Roman bricks and tufa worked into the fabric is sufficient to explain the theory of a Roman origin. In the early part of the thirteenth century the internal appearance of the church was altered a good deal by the addition of Early English work. As the centuries passed the building fell into decay, and Buck's engraving of 1735 shows it to be no more than a ruin, probably more picturesque to our romantic eyes than to those of the Age of Reason. At all events, in that Century of Reason the building was sufficiently patched up to become the depot coal-store, and so it remained until the 1850's. The restoration of the church in 1860–62 was entrusted to Sir Gilbert Scott, R.A., but as the guide-notes very fairly point out, it was not he who was responsible, twenty years later, for the " decorative mosaics applied to the walls "; the effect of that application each visitor will painfully judge for himself.

In spite of its interior decoration and its glass, St. Mary-within-the-Castle is a church of quite exceptional interest. The double-splayed windows in the nave, the built-up door in the south wall, and the great east and west arches of the tower are of Saxon work, though restored. The north and south arches of the tower, the lancet windows in the chancel, the groined vaults of the chancel and tower, and the fine piscina and sedile are part of the early thirteenth century alterations. The small window in the west wall enabled the guard to see, without entering the church, that the light was burning beside the altar in the south-east corner of the nave, which was used daily for the soldiers' mass. Also in the west wall, but high up and now replaced by a window, was a doorway giving access to some sort of gallery at the west end of the church, being connected on the outside with the pharos, which (under the appellation of the tower of " July Cæsar ") for long served as the belfry.

The earthwork which encloses the church and pharos was the first fortification on Castle Hill. It was King Harold's work

(1064–66), an oval enclosure surrounded by a ditch and an earth bank, topped by a wooden palisade. It was not until a hundred years later that masonry was first used, stone walls taking the place of the wooden palisades. But once the masons were called in, they quickly took control. The keep, a great cube of masonry nearly 100 feet each way, of unimaginable solidity and weight, was built about 1180, a few years after the curtain wall around the inner ward. The keep is approached by a forebuilding at the south-east corner, generally regarded as one of the best examples of its kind in England. The principal entrance, reached by the staircase in the forebuilding, is at second floor level. Just inside the main door is the well-chamber; the well shaft goes down 350 feet, but even at that depth is dry. On the same, that is, the second floor, are two great apartments, well furnished with specimens of arms and armour, and ceiled with modern brick vaults which were put in to take the weight of the water-tanks in the upper part of the tower. In the 20-foot thick walls are a number of small rooms, galleries and staircases which eventually lead on to the roof. It is not a difficult ascent (judged by ancient monument standards) and is well worth undertaking for the sake of the view from the roof— a view which embraces the Castle, the town, the harbour, the Channel, and, if the day is propitious, the French coast.

Most of the other buildings in the inner ward are modern, many of unfanciful R.E. architectural style (though the curious visitor will notice that in the range of buildings on the west side the usual prosaic twofold division for public purposes is replaced by the whimsical triple classification of " military," " civilians " and " ladies "), but the Palace Gate, on the south side, and the King's Gate, on the north, are of twelfth century construction, with alterations made at the time of the Napoleonic Wars. The entrance to the underground works, constructed in the solid chalk at various times between the year 1200 and 1945, is just to the north of the King's Gate.

The outer curtain wall, with its numerous towers and turrets, belongs to the middle of the thirteenth century. These towers in the outer wall range from the Constable's Gate, now the main entrance to the Castle and the Commanding Officer's residence, down to the watch towers capable of holding no more than a handful of men. Many of them bear the names of the Norman barons who held their lands on the particular form of military tenure known as Castle-guard: William de Averanche, Fulbert de Dover, William de Mamignot, William de Arsick, Robert de Porth, William Peverell, William de Crevequer and Adam FitzWilliam between them provided five knights, with their men-at-arms, throughout the year. The Constable also had to find five knights, so the total garrison consisted of the modest complement of ten knights supported by their men-at-arms.

The duties of the garrison, and the regulations governing the Castle, were set out at length in the " Statutes of Dover Castle " promulgated by Stephen de Pencestre, Constable and Warden from 1265 to 1298, who sought to bring some sort of order into the administrative vagueness which characterised both the Castle and the Ports. The Statutes order that the bridge shall be drawn and the gates shut at sunset, and that twenty warders are to mount guard on the walls; a warder sleeping on duty is to lose his day's pay—2d.—because the warders have the Constable's leave to sleep as much as they like in the daytime; a sergeant finding a warder asleep shall take something from him, or cut off a piece of his garment, as evidence of his slothfulness; if the King comes unexpectedly in the night the great gates are not to be opened, but he is to be admitted, with a small retinue, through the postern in the north wall known as the King's Gate. Another document, a little later in date, prescribes the garrison's rations: each man is to receive daily a half-pound loaf of bread, half a gallon of biscuit, five pints of wine, either half a " mess " of beef, mutton or pork (a hog counted as twenty-four messes) or five herrings or half a cod, together with cheese and oatmeal. On modern standards this seems to be a pretty generous calorific intake.

For the most part Dover Castle has led a comparatively unwarlike life. Its successful defence by Hubert de Burgh in 1216 against the Dauphin of France and the rebellious English barons was perhaps the most important event in its history; if Dover had fallen, the whole course of English history might well have been changed. But the Castle was unable to protect the town against a French raid in 1337, when the Priory was plundered and the borough charters were carried off. It fell into a state of neglect, which was aggravated by an earthquake that in 1580 caused part of the cliff and of the walls to collapse. Queen Elizabeth gave orders for the Castle to be repaired. It was perhaps about this time that " Queen Elizabeth's pocket pistol," a handsome gun 24 feet long, believed to have been presented to her by the States of Holland, was installed in the Castle in a position commanding the Straits. Unfortunately when, in 1635, a freebooter blockaded the harbour for several days, neither this piece of ordnance, nor any other, was capable of being fired from the Castle, and the blockade proceeded unmolested by any shore battery. At the beginning of the Civil War the Castle was held for the King, but in 1642 a small party of Parliamentarian Dovorians scaled the cliff, overcame the guard, and took prisoner the rest of the garrison—a less difficult feat than it sounds, for the guard consisted of four men, and the whole garrison of only twenty. For the remainder of the Commonwealth the Castle was held for Parliament, until in 1660 General Monk submitted it to the Earl of Winchelsea for the King. By then it was in a ruinous state, and so it remained until repairs were seriously taken in hand in the middle of the eighteenth century. During the War of American Independence, when France and Spain sided with the seceding colonists, and again during the war with Napoleonic France, the Castle was enlarged and strengthened. In 1800 it carried the formidable armament of 211 cannon. Further enlargement, but only by way of married quarters, took place in the second half of the nineteenth century; the additional defensive works belonging to the 1939–45 period are less conspicuous, except for a large spoil-tip at the foot of the cliff. That the Castle should have escaped practically unscathed after five years in Britain's front line is little short of a miracle.

Save for an aeroplane, the roof of the Castle keep is the best place from which to get a bird's-eye view of the town. It lies shut in by steep hills, running back inland for a couple of miles or more and spreading westward up the lateral valleys that carry the roads to Folkestone and St. Radigund's Abbey.

15 HASTINGS : Pelham Crescent

From an engraving by W. Westall, c. 1825.

16 DOVER : St. James's Street

From an engraving by George Shepherd, c. 1820.

17 THE CONSTABLE'S GATE in the Outer Ward, the main
entrance to Dover Castle

Seen from the sea or from the Admiralty Pier, the town can still be aptly described in Dickens' words: "The little narrow, crooked town of Dover hid itself away from the beach, and ran its head into the chalk cliffs, like a marine ostrich." It must have appeared very different to Julius Cæsar when he made his first landfall in Britain on that morning in August 2,000 years ago. Then the haven at Dover ran back between the hills to a point at least as far inland as the present Market Square. All that part of the town between the Market Square and the sea stands on land which is the slow accretion of centuries, an accretion that is partly the result of natural causes, but still more due to the extensive works which have been undertaken from time to time to construct, or preserve, a harbour at Dover.

The history of Roman Dover is still obscure, though excavation made possible by the devastation caused in the late war has enabled us to add to our knowledge of it. When the parish church of St. Mary the Virgin was rebuilt in the 1840's, a system of Roman baths was found beneath the west end, and forty years later traces of the same, or another, set of baths were found on the west side of the Market Square. It was here that the charming Roman statue, perhaps of a river-goddess, now to be seen in Dover Museum, was found. Another piece of sculpture, the head of a man, also now in the Museum, was found near the Market Square, and there have been many finds of smaller objects, but the exact position of the Roman fort which, with those at Richborough, Reculver and Lympne, formed part of the defence system of the Saxon Shore, remains conjectural. There is some, though scanty, evidence that it may have stood about where Church Street now turns northward out of the Square. In that position it would command the Roman haven, formed by the estuary of the Dour and now covered by Russell Street and St. James' Street (16).

Soon after the arrival of St. Augustine's mission, a band of monks was installed by Eadbald in "Dover Castle," that is, the old Roman fort by the haven, not the Castle on the hill. At the beginning of the eighth century Wihthred removed them to the new monastery of St. Martin-le-Grand, on the west side of what is now Market Square, and about 1135 they were removed again, to the Priory of St. Mary and St. Martin in the Newark. The fine Norman church built on the site of St. Martin-le-Grand was dismantled in 1540, but the ruins, towering over the Market Place, were not finally pulled down until 1881.

The town wall was long thought to be of Roman origin—the fact that two of the gates in it bore the names of Hadrian's Gate and Severus' Gate may, in part, have accounted for this theory—but, in fact, it was of medieval construction. Little of it now remains, though the line of the wall, with its ten gates, can partly be traced from street names—Townwall Street, Snargate Street, Adrian's Street and Cowgate Cemetery. It was built during the fourteenth century, like the walls at other Cinque Ports, to protect the town against the ravages of the French. The first record of a wall-tax granted to the barons of Dover is in 1346; it was followed by others in 1372, 1377 and 1380.

But even more than the building and repair of the town wall, the construction and constant reconstruction of the harbour occupied the energies of Dover for centuries. Already, by the year 1400, the Dour estuary was becoming choked with shingle, and through the breaching of the sea wall the town suffered repeated inundation. In 1474 and 1481 the King granted the town tolls on shipping and merchandise to enable the walls and harbour to be repaired. Towards the end of the same century a pier was built, to the design of John Clark, Master of the Maison Dieu, running out to sea from the western beach and forming a haven to which grateful Dover mariners gave the name Paradise. However, in 1530 the pier was partly destroyed and the harbour again became choked with beach. In the 1530's further extensive, and costly, works were carried out, but the south-westerly gales and the eastward drift of the shingle made it so difficult a job that the clerk of the works writes dispiritedly to his master: " Here hath been since your departure I suppose the devil, the works are sore spoiled, especially the west pier." Henry VIII took a keen personal interest in the work, but for all that it was a failure; in 1541 it was reported that already a bar of shingle had formed across the mouth of the harbour, and Camden, writing in 1586, says: " The town . . .

is more noted for the convenience of its harbour (though it has but little of that left it) and the passage from thence to France, than either its neatness or populousness." Still more extensive works were undertaken during the 1580's, with the aid of tolls granted to the town, but the problem of keeping the entrance to the haven clear of shingle was not solved. The revival in 1676 of the ancient custom of requiring every burgess, on the beating of a drum, to repair to the harbour with a shovel to clear away the shingle which accumulated after every storm, sounds like an intelligent anticipation of

> " If seven maids with seven mops
>   Swept it for half a year,
> Do you suppose," the Walrus said,
>   " That they could get it clear ? "
> " I doubt it," said the Carpenter,
>   And shed a bitter tear.

The harbour certainly continued to be the cause of bitter tears. By the time of Charles II the accumulation of silt had transformed Paradise into a marsh. Nowadays it is firm land, and Limekiln Street runs across it. At the beginning of the eighteenth century further statutes were enacted levying a toll on every ship passing Dover for the reparation of the harbour, but although much money was spent little good came of it. The method then in use for clearing the shingle-bar from the harbour mouth was to dam back the water at the mouth of the Dour, and then suddenly to release it, in the hope that it would cut through the bank of shingle. Sometimes it was successful, often not. Further work carried out at the end of the eighteenth century proved more effective than earlier attempts, and in 1792 a Dutch East Indiaman of 800 tons was able to enter the harbour. This was by no means the end of the story. At several periods during the next century improvements were made, and Wellington and Granville Docks then took their present form. The Admiralty Pier was finished in 1871, and was lengthened to 4,000 feet in the early years of the twentieth century, as part of the great scheme for enclosing Dover Bay as a harbour capable of receiving the largest warships. The making of this harbour—

not, of course, to be confused with the historic Dover Harbour—involved the building of three miles of deep sea masonry. As a harbour for battleships it is presumably now out of date, but the piers offer a magnificent marine promenade.

Even during the long periods when the harbour was giving trouble, Dover remained important as the most convenient port of passage to France. Domesday Book recorded the charges which the king's messenger was to pay for " transfretation "—3d. for each horse in the winter and 2d. in the summer. Henry III ordained that no one should cross the Channel to any port but Dover and pilgrims were later forbidden to leave England from any other port. This traffic was a profitable source of revenue to the town. In the reign of Edward III the tariff for passage across the Straits was fixed at 2s. 0d. for a horseman and 6d. for a footman. Dover has seen many notable arrivals and departures. It was here that Henry V landed on returning from his victorious campaigns in France; it was to Dover that Charles I came to meet Henrietta Maria, to whom he had been married by proxy; and it was at Dover that his son, Charles II, landed after his long involuntary exile, to be greeted with the Corporation's gift of a bible.

The wars in which England became engaged in the latter part of the eighteenth century for long cast a threat of invasion over the south-east coast, and defensive measures were taken. In 1779 three 28-gun batteries were constructed on the shore at Dover, and the first earthworks were thrown up on the Western Heights. A few years later Dover became the headquarters of the first battalion of the newly raised force of Cinque Ports' Fencible Cavalry; the regiment was disbanded after the Battle of Waterloo. In 1802 the Shaft Barracks and the Grand Shaft Staircase (which, cut through the solid chalk, leads from Snargate Street to the heights above) were built.

Fortunately these defensive measures never had to be put to the test, and Dover was able to develop peacefully into an early nineteenth century watering-place. The elegant Waterloo Crescent (13) and the once handsome but now bedraggled houses along Marine Parade belong to this phase of Dover's history. To the early Victorian family seeking a thoroughly respectable but healthy seaside holiday, nothing could have been more eligible than an apartment in one of these houses over-looking the Straits. It is sad that they suffered so badly during the war; it is melancholy, too, that the planners, in healing the war-time scars, have proposed to perform a plastic surgical operation and to give Dover a new face, for they would like "to demolish the poor type Regency buildings on the Sea Front" (having been built in 1824 they are of "obsolete design") "and to erect in their stead blocks of flats and residential hotels of high quality, six and eight storeys in height, upon a new building line, some 180 feet inshore, and to lay out the intervening space between these buildings and the existing promenade as lawns and gardens." But it seems likely that the six- and eight-storey blocks of flats and hotels will have to be put off for a while, and if the poor type Regency buildings, of obsolete design, are to have a few years' respite, not everyone will be sorry.

It must be admitted that, except for the Castle, Dover is not rich in secular buildings of distinction. Few examples of architecture such as one thinks of as being typical of the Cinque Ports have here survived. Most of the houses and shops were built in the nineteenth century (the population increased from about 8,000 in 1800 to about 40,000 in 1900), and although the rows of terrace-houses, with their purple slated roofs, make felicitous patterns when seen from the heights of Castle Hill, many of these modern streets, seen at close quarters, suffer from excessive by-law regularity.

One handsome red-brick building, which is scarcely likely to escape attention, is Maison Dieu House in Biggin Street. Built in 1665, and for long the residence of the Admiralty Victualling Agent, it now belongs to the Corporation, and is fittingly to become the Public Library. But another house, perhaps the prettiest in Dover, is likely to be overlooked—Laurieston House, an early nineteenth century building of modest size, which rests halfway up the slope on the east side of the town, close to the imposing terrace known as Victoria Park. Laurieston House is surrounded by an exquisitely proportioned verandah, specially designed, one would think, as a setting to show off Jane Austen heroines—or, unhappily, *was* surrounded would perhaps be more accurate, for the house, like many others in Dover, suffered sorely during the war, and has fallen into a sad state of decay.

Adjacent to Maison Dieu House is the Maison Dieu itself, a hospital founded in 1203 by Hubert de Burgh for the accommodation of pilgrims, most of them no doubt passing through Dover on their way to or from the Shrine of St. Thomas of Canterbury. Later it was used for sick and maimed soldiers returning from the continent. The existing Great Hall underwent restoration in the 1850's, and the Council Chamber was added in 1868. The Connaught Hall (1883), a plush-adorned cavern wherein respectability and gloom lie embalmed together, opens out on the west side of the Great Hall. The Maison Dieu Hall, with the restored traces of the infirmary chapel (open to the public) and the Council Chamber (usually to be seen, when not in use, on application to the Town Sergeant), contain a number of pictures of local interest, particularly those in the Sandeman Collection, and some of general interest, including portraits of Queen Elizabeth, of Queen Anne by Kneller, and of Eve by (reputedly) Lucas Cranach. The windows are a salutary reminder that not all Victorian stained glass is to be despised. The Hall also contains colours worked by Dover ladies for the volunteers called out at the time of the Napoleonic scare. It is well furnished with arms and armour, as is also the well-arranged Museum situated beneath the Connaught Hall. Indeed, the visitor, remembering also the fine collection at the Castle, is likely to be impressed with the obvious belligerency of bygone Dover, so in fairness it should be added that some of the objects are on loan from the Tower of London Armouries.

Amongst other interesting exhibits, the Museum contains some of the Corporation plate and insignia. Especially noteworthy is the burghmote horn made of latten by John of Germany (so it is inscribed) probably in the thirteenth century. It was used for calling together the common assembly for the annual election of the mayor or for any other special business. The Hohler etchings give some idea of the way in which the town of Dover has evolved; the eel spears are an interesting relic of the days when the waters of the Dour were pure enough to support aquatic life.

On the opposite side of Biggin Street from the Maison Dieu, and lying between Biggin Street and Priory Road, is a small stone building, revealed to public view by the destruction of buildings in Priory Road. Formerly it was the Chapel of St. Edmund, to whom it was dedicated on its erection in 1253, and, with its burial-ground, it belonged to the Maison Dieu. Man has dealt more hardly with the little chapel than has Time. It is now to be rescued from the ignominy into which it has fallen, and is to " be preserved amid lawns and gardens."

To the west of this little wayside chapel lay the Priory of St. Martin and St. Mary Newark. The original priory of St. Martin-le-Grand, as we have said, occupied a site near the present-day Market Square. In Henry I's reign the canons of the Priory, accused of behaving with gross irregularity, got so out of hand that the King granted Dover Priory to the Archbishop of Canterbury and Christchurch Priory. The Archbishop, William de Corbeuil, promptly ejected all the secular canons and began to build the new Priory outside the then limits of the town. The great church, cruciform in shape, was something like 285 feet in length, and from north to south the transepts measured 155 feet. In 1845 it was destroyed to make way for building operations; Saxon Street and Effingham Street now obliterate all trace of its site. Of the conventual buildings, three remain, all now part of Dover College: the Refectory, backing on to Effingham Street, the Priory Gate, and the King's Chamber, which has become the College Chapel. By the entrance to the College, in St. Martin's Street, the College authorities have thoughtfully provided a plan which shows the position of the surviving Priory buildings.

Farther along Biggin Street, and within the line of the medieval town wall, is the parish church of St. Mary the Virgin. Except for the tower, it was almost entirely taken down and rebuilt in 1843. The Norman tower consists of five stages—the west door, a triple low arcade, and above that three graceful slender-shafted arcades. It was found, during the 1843 rebuilding operations, that the string course between the two lower and the upper three stages marks a division between what are, n effect, two separate buildings; the three upper stages simply stand upon the two lower: the workmanship and materials are different, and there is no bonding of the stonework. High up on the south side of the tower is a good seventeenth century sundial. Although the present clock is less than a hundred years old, St. Mary's has had a clock since the town clock was set up there in 1539, when the old church of St. Martin-le-Grand was dismantled.

The interior of the church is made somewhat dark by the two great galleries. That on the north side contains the seats of the Mayor and Corporation. Earlier the Mayor, Corporation and Jurats sat in a pew of their own behind the altar. Charles II, visiting the town in 1670, objected to the practice, and ordered the doors of the pew to be nailed up. It seems to have remained unused for some time, but a generation later the Mayor and Corporation had found their way back to their accustomed seats, in spite of the protests of the churchwardens. In 1805 the churchwardens commenced an action against the Corporation, but found that litigation was an expensive luxury they could not afford. Finally, in 1836 the Mayor and Corporation agreed " to discontinue the indecent practice of sitting round the Altar " and were given the seats that they still occupy. In front of the Mayor's seat is a fine royal coat of arms of the reign of William and Mary, with William's personal motto *Jay Mien Tend Ray (Je maintiendrai)*. It was in St. Mary's that the Mayor used to be elected every year; the freemen were assembled by the blowing of the common horn, a proclamation was made, and those not free were warned to depart upon pain of losing their upper garments.

In the corresponding gallery on the south side of the church the pilots, who have revived the practice of attending church as a body on Trinity Sunday, have their seats. The Pilots of the Cinque Ports erected their own gallery over the west door in 1698, and moved to their present position when the church was rebuilt in 1843. Since 1948 the coat of arms of the Master and Brethren of Trinity House, Deptford Strond, has been displayed on the front of the Pilots' Gallery. The Cinque

Ports Pilots ceased to be a separate body, and were reorganised under the jurisdiction of Trinity House, Deptford Strond, in 1853. For at least 300 years before that they had been a self-governing body, with their " elder brethren " and " younger brethren," making and enforcing their own rules in their Court of Lodemanage, which met in old St. James' Church, now, alas! a chance victim of the 1939–45 war.

Two nearly contemporary, but contrasting, wall tablets are worth noting. That to Peter Eaton, who died in 1769, is on the west wall, a large monument incorporating an incongruous and surrealistic variety of objects—the work of an eighteenth century Salvador Dali in stone. The other is beside the south door, a tablet to Charles Churchill, poet and satirist, who died at Boulogne in 1764 and was buried at Dover. Churchill was a dissipated libertine and has a charming and chaste memorial; Eaton was a highly virtuous man. This strangely ill-assorted pair, whose dust lies commingled with the soil of Dover, may stand for a symbol, in a way, of the town itself, for its essence is its odd admixture of diversities, of respectability and decorum with vulgarity and fun; perhaps therein lies Dover's charm, which only too probably has after all escaped our analytical and descriptive verbal net.

THE BRASEN HORNE OF SAYLENCE

CHAPTER IV

SANDWICH

SANDWICH, like Rye, combines a great and historical past with a present picturesque quality which is at once gracious and intimate in its appeal. The two towns, moreover, have much more in common than this charm of sentiment. Both stood on tidal rivers which, by reason of great changes in the face of the land and the line of the sea-coast, were obliged to change their courses; each town, once a busy and flourishing seaside port, was stranded inland with but a fraction of its former maritime connection, and no opportunity, as had some of the other Ports, to develop into a modern watering-place. Rye and Sandwich are also walled towns, and they have the strong individual characters which are so often the mark of boroughs circumscribed in that way.

The especial appeal and attraction of Sandwich is due to this deep sense of local unity which has fashioned its spirit as well as its topography, and given it a time-tested native quality graced by outlandish names and by architectural forms which have become merged in the vernacular. Within it of all places the evidence tells plainly of the peacefully developed culture of a small English town which was little disturbed by the violent events of the outside world. But before speaking of its present charm, we ought to say a little of the early history of Sandwich and its haven which, until the Norman Conquest, was rated as the foremost port of England. Its annals have been very fully collated in the massive work of William Boys, a local surgeon, *Collections for a History of Sandwich*, published in 1792.

The name of the place probably means market town on sandy soil, and it was so known at least by the middle years of the ninth century, by which time it had become the counterpart of the much earlier and then decayed Roman port of Richborough. Its very great maritime importance is shown by the repeated attention paid to it from this time until the early part of the eleventh century by Scandinavian sea-rovers, the Norwegians, Swedes and Danes, known collectively as the Vikings. The frequent use of its roadstead by English and Vikings alike is evidence of its strategic value; it can never have been completely sacked, and its prosperity may have been due in some measure to an admixture of Viking blood with that of the Saxon inhabitants. It was the early mustering-place of the fleets of England, and its well-being was further assured by Canute, who in 1029 granted or restored the town to the monastery of Christ Church, Canterbury, with which great body its government and revenues remained until the Dissolution of the Monasteries.

An indication of the standing of Sandwich is given by the record in Domesday. It was in itself a hundred; it contained the large number of 383 houses, and it rendered to the King ship service with twenty ships on the same terms as Dover. It was the second largest town in Kent, and seems to have been the seventh in order of size in England. The interests of Sandwich were closely allied to those of Dover, not only in ship-service to the Crown, but also in the regulation of the all-important North Sea herring fishery, in which industry the men of Sandwich had been engaged before the Conquest, and it seems likely that some sort of association may have been evolved to further their common purpose.

The early importance of the place is evident enough from the illustrious names associated with it. In 1194 Richard I landed at Sandwich and walked to Canterbury as a thanksgiving for his deliverance from Austria; it was used constantly by the English fleets under Edward III, particularly for Crecy and for the siege of Calais, to which expedition it contributed twenty-two ships and 504 men; after Poictiers, the Black Prince landed here in 1357 with his prisoner, the King of France; in 1475 Edward IV embarked at Sandwich for Calais " with one of the finest armies that had ever passed from Britain to the continent "; and so its fame continues with a memorable visit of Elizabeth on her progress in 1572 (houses in Strand Street were to be beautified and adorned with black and white, streets were to be paved and all dung removed or covered, brewers must brew good beer against her coming and butchers must carry their offal to the furthest groyne-head, 200 persons were to be apparelled in white doublets, black gallygascoignes and white garters, while children were to spin yarn on scaffolds hung with black-and-white baize), a visit of Cromwell in 1651, and of Charles II's queen, Catherine of Braganza, the Infanta of Portugal, who would not stop for her banquet. Less pleasant visitations were those of the French, who sacked the town in 1216, and twice again before a final assault in 1456.

Throughout the Middle Ages Sandwich maintained an enviable place in the confederation of the Cinque Ports, of which it was for a time the first in prosperity. Its trade flourished, and its seamen, like those of the other Ports, were not over scrupulous when it came to piracy and wrecking as a profitable sideline to legitimate ship-service. One incident, in 1305, is a measure of others. The *Snake* of Sandwich, which was patrolling the Strait of Dover under royal orders for the better security of merchantmen, boarded a London ship, one of those which should have fallen to its care, and lifted part of its cargo, together with £250 in specie. After the decline of Winchelsea and Rye, Sandwich came into further prominence. Not only did it have thereby an increased trade, but its neighbour and rival port of Stonar did not recover from a great inundation of the sea in 1365, when all the marshes between Canterbury and the mouth of the Stour were in danger of being drowned. Still further prestige and trade came to the town with the removal thither in 1377 of the wool staple from Queenborough, while its haven served as a convenient anchorage and supply depot to both naval and merchant craft, two functions which by the seventeenth century had become the accepted business of the Downs and the port of Deal.

Long before the seventeenth century, however, the port of Sandwich had passed its heyday. Its decay was due to the interplay of several causes, natural and artificial. The chief was certainly the deposition of very large quantities of sand and silt in the area where the Channel tides met those of the North Sea, while this natural blockage was assisted by the formation of shoals against the wrecks of one or more fair-sized ships in the haven itself. Of the precise identity of these wrecked ships

18   RAMPART OF THE TOWN WALL

19   THE BARBICAN OR BRIDGE GATE

SANDWICH

20   THE CHURCH OF ST. CLEMENT with its elaborate Norman Tower, Sandwich

there is some doubt. Leland, who visited the town during his Itinerary between 1536 and 1542, wrote that " The caryke that was sonke yn the haven yn Pope Paulus tyme did much hurt to the haven, and gether a great banke "—it is thought that his reference was to Paul II (1464–71)—and there is reference in Boys' Annals to the wreck of a Spanish ship outside Richborough which was to be removed in 1483; five years later the Mayor was given £40 for raising a ship of 120 tons which was blocking the haven. The natural silting of the haven was part of the geological process which was responsible for the formation of the Goodwin Sands, and it was encouraged by the inning and draining of the marshlands of the Wantsum and the Lower Stour, which was undertaken largely at the instance of the chief landowners, the two great monastic houses at Canterbury. It was the land water, drained into new channels, which upset a condition of uneasy geological balance, and in the end lost the town its once famous harbour. There was, in the meantime, some little trade. In 1566 the port could boast seventeen ships, including one of 40 tons, and sixty-two men; in 1628 there were sixteen ships, ten of under 100 tons burthen, ten boys and seventy-eight men, but in 1637 when the Cinque Ports petitioned for special exemption in the provision of ship-money, the haven was said to be silting up and the port had nothing beyond a trade in coal and corn with London. Now the little town is stranded some two miles from the sea, and its waterborne traffic consists of an occasional barge laden with coke, cement or timber, and from time to time a cabin cruiser finds its way to moorings at the Quay near Barbican Gate.

The fortunes of the town and its neighbourhood were somewhat revived just after the middle of the sixteenth century by the settlement under the Queen's direct patronage of French and Flemish families who had fled from religious persecution in their own countries. These " gentle strangers " were skilled in market gardening; they grew vegetables, and particularly carrots, in the fine sandy soil, and other of their brethren, encouraged by the inhabitants of the town, set up a prosperous trade in baize and flannel. On the economic side, Sandwich felt a considerable benefit, for rents rose with the expanding trade. The refugees, too, introduced a pleasant style of domestic building in brick, with a characteristic form of gable which spread quickly in East Kent; the Dutch House in King Street (21), and The Whitefriars, once the home of William Boys, are two delightful examples of this brick building in Sandwich itself. In 1588 a potter from Delft was permitted to settle and carry on his business in the town.

Any topographical account of Sandwich ought to start with the walls. There was a stone wall on the west side, but earthen ramparts bounded the other three sides of a rectangular plan, and as Mill Wall, Rope Walk and The Butts they still continue as pleasant tree-lined walks above the course of the town ditch (18). Two of the original five gates still remain. The Barbican (19), with its picturesque flanking bastions, now controls the toll bridge over the Stour and the road to Thanet, and Fisher Gate (22), which was in existence by 1457, though the present gateway with its portcullis grooves is dated 1571, overlooked the ferry which, before the bridge, carried the Thanet traffic.

It is uncertain how much of Sandwich was destroyed in the French raids, but its narrow and twisted streets, the courses of which are clearly to be seen from the top of St. Clement's Church tower, still contain many old and picturesque houses (23). Some are timber-framed, others built of mellow local brick, the raw material for which was mud from the haven. Often an early Georgian front, severe and economical in its detail, covers a house which is in the main Tudor or Jacobean. The most interesting are Manwood Court, a fine Elizabethan house built in 1564 as a grammar school; the Old House on the bank of the Stour where traditionally Elizabeth stayed during her visit to Sandwich; Flint House in High Street, the knapped flintwork of which hides an early house; and the Custom House, 19 Strand Street, which has a finely executed coat of arms of James I in painted plaster, and remarkable plaster ceilings.

There are three ancient churches within the walls. The scene is dominated by St. Peter's, a thirteenth century fabric with a far-seen bulbous cupola, which stands in the middle of the town. The feature of greatest interest, apart from the bone-crypt, is the three fine medieval tombs in recesses which project beyond the wall of the north aisle, the deliberate mutilation of which makes any attempt at their attribution sheer guess-work. The upper part of the tower of this church was rebuilt of Sandwich brick after its collapse in 1661. Prominent, too, is the massive central tower of St. Clement's (20), in an advanced Norman style with external wall-arcades. A remarkable fitting in this church is an early fifteenth century font, the naturalistic and heraldic carving on the stem of which is a fine example of contemporary art. The Church of St. Mary was rebuilt in its present barn-like form after the fall of its tower and spire in 1667. Both it and St. Peter's have tall narrow reliquaries in the chancel. A notable sixteenth century chalice is still in use. At St. Clement's there are other fine pieces of church plate, which include a Georgian bowl, a christening basin, the gift of the Town Midwife, whose office was executed " by the Divine Assistance with Generall Aprobation & Success."

Outside the walls and just beyond the railway station is the beautiful and interesting chapel of St. Bartholomew's Hospital, which was probably founded early in the thirteenth century. The Hospital has been very much restored, and the chief domestic offices have disappeared; it has a direct Cinque Port interest in the tomb and mailed figure of a Lord Warden, Sir Henry de Sandwich, who died in 1244. There were three other medieval hospitals in Sandwich, but no remains of them are left. The Carmelite Friars founded a house here in 1272, and its site which is now indicated by Whitefriars in New Street was excavated in recent years, and the plan of the church and convent buildings recovered.

Of particular interest is the Guildhall in the cobbled Market Square. It was built in 1578 and, in spite of its modern over-restored exterior, much of the original framework is still evident. The Town Sergeant insists upon his right to conduct visitors round the Court Hall and Council Chamber, and explains in detail the panelled jury-box, the halberds of the Cinque Ports fleet, the heraldic wooden carvings made especially as an ornament to one of the Town Gates for Queen Elizabeth's visit in 1572, the various pictures and the massive wooden thumb-press. The framed Charter of Charles II in the Mayor's Parlour is only one of an extensive series of valuable and well-kept historical records. Such is the principal public building of townsmen of whom it was said that " their frequent intercourse with strangers rendered them respectable in their manners, and their acquired knowledge of trade eminently qualified them to give advice in all matters of commerce."

The Thanet road out of Sandwich crosses a wide level of reclaimed marshland. Away to the west, the Saxon Shore fort called Richborough Castle rears its great bulk against the skyline; there it has stood for 1,600 years, the witness of some of the most famous events in English history. Look at the romantic names in German Text type on the Ordnance Survey Map—St. Augustine's Well, the site of the oak under which he sat, the Boarded Groin, which is an embankment made to exclude the sea after the great inundation of 1364, and Ebbsfleet, the site of the landing of Hengist and Horsa in 449, as well as of St. Augustine and his Christian missionaries in 597. The Saint is commemorated by a modern copy of a Celtic cross set up in 1884 and already weathering badly, the sinners by the Hugin, a replica of a Viking long-ship which sailed from Denmark to Britain to mark the 1,500th anniversary of the Saxon landing, and which is now at its last berth, a concrete cradle on the gentle slope of the shore overlooking Pegwell Bay.

At Stonar Cut, a channel some 600 feet in length made in 1775 across the parallel courses of the River Stour, between the river itself and Sandwich Haven, to save the tortuous journey by the normal course of the river, we come across a clue to the medieval town of Stonar, once a limb of Sandwich. It is no longer even a village, and the ridge of flint shingle on which it stood is being slowly quarried away; Stonar Lake provided ballast to make the Admiralty Harbour at Dover, and its flint pebbles may have provided the glaze on your tea-cup. At the top of their great flooded pit, the Wingham Engineering Company have found pottery, knives, hones and keys—the everyday odds and ends of the inhabitants of this long-forgotten town, an outport of London which never recovered from a sack by the French in 1385, from recurrent flooding, and from the choking

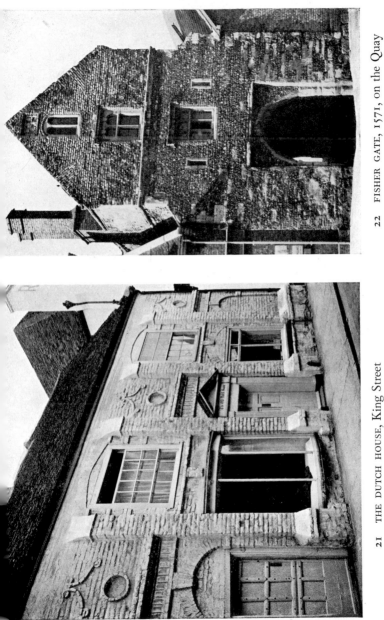

21 THE DUTCH HOUSE, King Street

22 FISHER GATE, 1571, on the Quay

SANDWICH

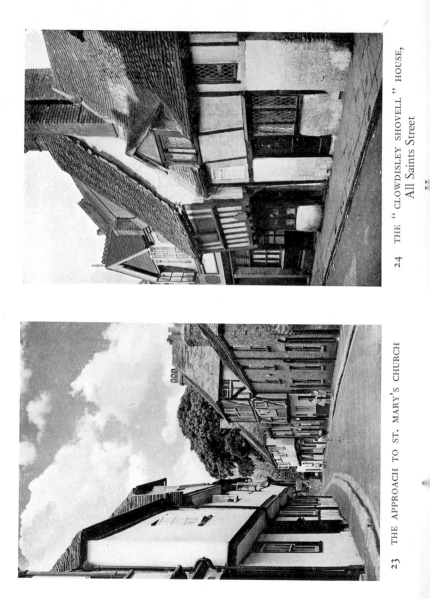

23　THE APPROACH TO ST. MARY'S CHURCH

24　THE "CLOWDISLEY SHOVELL" HOUSE,
All Saints Street

by sand which was caused by the geographical changes of this unstable coast. It had been a limb of Sandwich since about 1206, and on its decline trade went to its prosperous rival.

Richborough, near neighbour to Stonar, and in fact part of it, became in the First World War a " Mystery Port," a naval base from which a train-ferry carried vast supplies of arms to the continent. The wreck and ruin of its later activities is strewn over the marshland landscape. A section of a Mulberry Harbour—appropriately enough it reminds us of the prefabricated palisade of wood with which the French intended to invest a strongpoint on the English coast, a structure which was captured in 1385 and set up at Sandwich—together with locomotives, tanks and trucks, strange masses of concrete and rails and girders, makes an exciting backcloth set in the feeble light of a waning October moon. Now it is a seat of light industry—hot-water bottles and other rubber goods, dolls which cry, and sewing machines—with the yellow and blue caravans of dour and sullen gypsies parked for the night in the vacant lots.

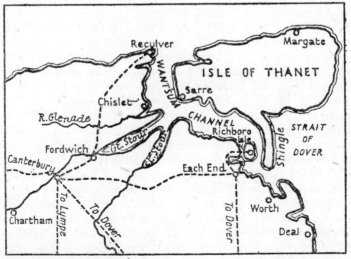

From Chartham to Deal is 16¾ miles

THE WANTSUM CHANNEL BEFORE THE FOUNDATION OF SANDWICH

CHAPTER V

ROMNEY

THE Port of Romney, with its corporate member of Lydd and its non-corporate members of Broomhill, Old Romney Dengemarsh and Oswaldstone, lies wholly in Romney Marsh. Its history at all times has closely followed the natural evolution and artificial development of the Marsh, processes which were far from simple, and, although from a constitutional point of view, New Romney must always be regarded as in the Marsh but not of it, it is nevertheless against the background of what Richard Barham in the *Ingoldsby Legends* calls the fifth quarter of the globe that its life may best be seen.

The name of Romney Marsh is properly and exactly given to the land northward and eastward of the Rhee Wall, which was reclaimed and put under cultivation in Roman times. The Wall, a remarkable piece of Roman civil engineering, consisted of a large drainage channel, by which the main waters of the River Rother were boldly carried from the neighbourhood of Appledore south-eastward to Romney and to the sea, instead of being allowed to follow their former course and reach the sea near Hythe; the channel was furnished with an embankment on each side, and probably at a very early date—the channel was silted up by the end of the fourteenth century—the Wall carried a predecessor of the existing road from Appledore by Snargate and Brenzett to Old and New Romney. In course of time this region of rich marshland evolved its own peculiar system of local law and government, and it was for this area that rules and ordinances for the keeping of embankments and waterways and the principles of land drainage, and possibly for coastal protection against the ravages of the sea, were first enacted in Britain. The ordinances of Henry de Bathe made in 1258 became models of their kind; the first Kentish topographer, Lambarde, wrote in 1570, that " Experience in time hath begotten such Allowance and liking that . . . they are now become a Pattern to all like Places in the whole Realm. . . ."

25 NEW ROMNEY : sheep graze where once the sea flowed

26 HIGH STREET, with
its Elizabethan and
Georgian fronts

27 THE   PINNACLED
NORMAN TOWER OF
ST. NICHOLAS, one
of the noblest among
the   Cinque   Port
churches

NEW ROMNEY

Two famous Corporations and their predecessors—the Lords, Bailiff and Jurats of Romney Marsh, and the Bailiff, Jurats and Commonalty of Romney Marsh—administered the affairs of the 24,000 acres of the Level and Liberty of Romney Marsh at least from the thirteenth century until the recent establishment of Catchment Boards.

It will be readily imagined that such well-established bodies did not always see eye to eye with their neighbours, the barons of the Cinque Ports of Hythe and New Romney, and the men of the Marsh had frequent and serious disputes with the Ports over such matters as embanking, and the building and repair of sluices.

By a popular understanding, Walland Marsh and Denge Marsh, both of which were in existence early in the Middle Ages, and the wide shingle spits of Dungeness Foreland are included under the name of Romney Marsh, though all lie to the westward of the Rhee Wall. In the widest terms, at its extreme western boundary are the towns of Winchelsea and Rye, each on its small hill; to the north-west is the stranded Isle of Oxney, and away inland are the Aldington Hills, the old line of cliffs which, at the time of the remote Neolithic Depression, the last land movement of any considerable moment in this part of Britain, was the seashore of Kent; below them is an artificial boundary to the Marsh in Pitt's Royal Military Canal; at the eastern extremity and beyond Dymchurch Wall, an ancient line of protective defence against the sea, which was put into its present form by Rennie in 1804, lies the hillside Cinque Port of Hythe.

So, nowadays, New Romney, once a flourishing port, is a mile and a quarter from the sea (25); Old Romney, with its Longport Wharf, is twice that distance inland, and Lydd isolated beyond vast marine shingle ridges. These paradoxes of history are the result of a complex series of changes in coastal erosion and aggradation (see map on p. 89).

The great level of Romney Marsh resulted from the denudation of the soft Weald Clay country, and the deposition of the sand and fine material brought down southward by many small streams upon a low-lying area which was itself slowly sinking in relation to the level of the sea. The building up and consolidation of this area into a marsh was encouraged by the protection which the great shingle mass of Dungeness gave from the sea. But much we are still uncertain about—for example, exactly where the Rother debouched near Hythe in Roman times, and the effect of reclamation south of the Rhee Wall between the ninth and thirteenth centuries by the land-owners, the successive Archbishops of Canterbury.

There were important changes in the face of the land during the eighth century. Charters of Eadbriht to Christ Church, Canterbury, in 741, and of Offa in 774, make it clear that the shingle of Dungeness was growing seawards; the harbour of Romney was already in existence, and the *Merscware*, the men of the Marsh, at that early date already had pastures for large flocks. The town of Lydd, on an island in the mouth of the Rother became stranded, and in 893 a Danish fleet of 250 ships passed it on the way up to Appledore. Equally important was the holding up at Dungeness of masses of shingle which would otherwise have drifted northward along the shore of East Road and Dymchurch Bay; the seaward edge of the Marsh had therefore in its turn to be given the protection of Dymchurch Wall.

In the twelfth and thirteenth centuries a slow depression of the land surface which had followed a rising during the Roman period, and the consequent cultivation of the Marsh by that people, allowed full effect to those natural catastrophes of which the sixteenth century chroniclers, Leland, Holinshed and Camden write so vividly. By reason of great storms and subsequent inundations of the sea, the original port of Win-chelsea was lost; the River Rother was diverted from its mouth at New Romney nearly to its present outfall at Rye; the whole coast-line of Romney Marsh developed a new configura-tion; and the port of Romney, which, unlike its fellow-ports of Dover and Sandwich, had no secondary means of securing its livelihood and now no river upon which to base even a meagre fishing industry, sank into decline. Its original service was for five ships, but later this was reduced to three and a half.

Its broken fortune was a little tempered by the fact that New Romney became the accepted meeting-place of the Court of

Brodhull or "Brotherhood," and it so kept in close touch with the pageantry and the constitutional proceedings of the Cinque Ports, at the same time becoming the repository for official records. These records, which are carefully preserved in the Cinque Ports Chest in the Town Hall and are open to inspection by appointment, include the White Book, which is the minute book of the Brodhull from 1433 to 1571, the Black Book, which is the minute book of the Brodhull and Guestling from 1572 until the present day, the very interesting Diaries of the Bailiffs at the Yarmouth herring-fishery fair from 1582 to 1639, and various lists of ships, letters, petitions, fines, and accounts. Of equal and complementary interest are the local records of Romney itself, which begin with the assessments of 1379 and contain an unsurpassed and detailed account of the life of a town through many centuries. Even earlier is the Register of Daniel Rough, Common Clerk of Romney from 1353 to 1380, now in the Library of St. Catharine's College, Cambridge. For long years there were disputes between the barons of Romney and their overlords, the Archbishops of Canterbury, concerning the encroachments of the ecclesiastics on the Cinque Port liberties, and it is ironical that the town was not granted the right to choose its own Mayor until the charter of Elizabeth in 1563, long after its day as an exalted member of the Confederation had passed.

The state of Romney in the reign of Henry VIII was thus described in the notes which John Leland left for his *Itinerary*:—

" Rumeney is one of the V. portes, and hath bene a metely good haven, yn so much that withyn remembrance of men shyppes have cum hard up to the towne, and cast ancres yn one of the chyrch yardes. The se is now a ii myles fro the towne, so sore therby now decayed that where ther wher iii. great paroches and chirches sumtyme is now scant one wel mayteined."

A chance meeting in New Romney with a workman who made the recent foundations of the bridge carrying Church Lane over Main Sewer brought Leland's reference up to date; here were dug out the remains of the beams of a wharf which once stood close by the churchyard.

It was not that the men of Romney were apathetic in trying to preserve what was left of their inheritance. There was new cutting and walling and sluicing in the fifteenth century, and before the middle years of the succeeding century they were wise enough to expend much money on reclaiming land which was formerly part of their harbour. The waterway to Appledore was already silted up, but they made views of levels and consulted with their neighbours and with Authority—even in 1488 considering the capture of water from Guldeford Level near Rye—in the hope of bringing prosperity back to their decayed haven. The " land between the walls," that is, the silted up channel of the Rhee, had by now been recognised as part of the liberty of the Cinque Port, and this long narrow belt of country again linked the former bay of Appledore with the haven at Romney. But it was of no avail; man could not, in this instance, triumph over Nature.

The manuscript records of the town mention one of its fascinating medieval traditions, that of the Romney Mystery Play. It was performed at Crockley Green on the southern side of the town from a script, *Le Playboke*, which was municipal property, and chiefly by members of the fraternities and guilds associated with religious and trade life. There were various plays in the book, many of them with sacred characters derived from the old miracle mysteries—The Resurrection and The Passion of Our Lord—but there were others which told of St. George and the Dragon, Father Christmas, the King of Egypt, the Turkish Knight and Giant Turpin. The players were often encouraged by gifts of wine, especially as they travelled the surrounding countryside with their show. John Craye and Thomas a'Nasshe were appointed Wardens of the Play, and in 1463 Agnes Ford was given a fee of 6s. 8d. for producing the Interlude of Our Lord's Passion; in 1503 special gear cost 3s. 4d. to bring from London. These are bare facts noted from the contemporary records, but we can well imagine the crowd of minstrels, jugglers, tricksters and familiars of these Marshland fairs, perhaps including even such another actor-turned-spy as Robert Gandelyn.

In its decay, says Samuel Jeake writing in 1678, New Romney

is " neither plentiful in Buildings nor Populous in people . . . though generally those that are, love to be as stately as most in Kent." The population was but 500 souls at one survey during the eighteenth century, but the Georgian-fronted houses in the High Street and the lines of Cobb's House, now fallen even below its standing when it served as the Workhouse, are evidence enough of its former dignity (26). Whole streets on the northern side of the town have disappeared; their tracks were still visible in the grass a century ago, but the speculative builder of the day preferred to turn his attention southward to the seashore and in 1886 he laid out Littlestone-on-Sea. A drawing of a pier for this " Eastbourne-that-might-have-been " may be seen in the Court Room of the Town Hall.

This room—it is a museum as much as a court—has maps and plans of great Cinque Ports interest, old seals of Romney and the town purse; it has coins and tokens of real historic value, the town pillory and stocks, a map of the sites in Kent where doodle-bugs crashed, and the usual invalided gallipots. But of more interest, perhaps, is the banner stretched across the whole of the east wall, a faded blue, red, and yellow flag, a Lord Warden's Banner; it was such a flag, with its quartered half-lions, demi-hulls, castles, crown and anchor and ship in full sail, that caused much speculation when it was worn in 1891 by a ship off Dover, so much that it could only be read as a somewhat unorthodox signal for " pilot required," and a man was accordingly sent off. The Lord Warden's Banner, which is now seen regularly at Chartwell, Westerham, was perhaps as much of a puzzle in 1950 to the people of St. Annes-on-Sea when it was flown at a hotel to mark the presence of Mr. Winston Churchill at the Conservative Party Conference. The Banner of the Cinque Ports, which was used on ceremonial occasions, particularly at the opening of the Yarmouth Free Fair, is to be seen in the Council Chamber of the Maison Dieu at Dover (4); the present banner, which has been most carefully repaired, was made about 1632. The sixteenth century " brasen horne of saylence," with which the Yarmouth Fair was proclaimed open, may also be seen in the Town Hall at New Romney (p. 63).

Of five medieval religious foundations in New Romney

there remains only the parish church of St. Nicholas (27), the grand Romanesque tower of which with its angle pinnacles and the stump of a former steeple is a far-seen landmark of the Marsh. The whole church—apart from the tower and the nave arcades it is nearly all well-designed Decorated of the latter half of the fourteenth century—has the atmosphere if not the absolute quality of an East Anglian wool-merchants' church. From very early times it was used for municipal and Cinque Port business; such a use down to modern times is recorded by the huge clock, presented by the Corporation in 1826 and converted later at its expense to an eight-day movement, and by the holding within the church in 1937 " as of old time accustomed " of the Courts of Brotherhood and Guestling. The tomb of Richard Stuppenye in the south aisle was long used as a table during the election of the Mayor; and there is a brass effigy of Thomas Lambard, 1514, who appeared for Romney in a deputation to the Brotherhood of 1506. The perpeyn screens with their sedilia, and the tomb-recess in the north chapel, which may be an Easter Sepulchre and possibly a reliquary, are interesting features of the church.

Fragments of Gothic and Tudor mouldings are built into the side garden wall of the house called St. John's Priory (28). Nothing is known of the foundation of the Hospital of St. John, which was conducted under the responsibility of the Jurats of the town, and it is likely that by the end of the fifteenth century the house was no longer in use as a hospital. It is hard to think charitably of a later owner who created an artificial ruin on its site.

For the rest, we must be content to recall the New Inn with its Georgian front masking the frame of a sixteenth (and perhaps fifteenth) century building, wherein there is good timber work and, in the dining-room, a delightful and well-proportioned Georgian glass cupboard, cream painted and metal-backed. At the corner of Cannon Street and Stonehouse Road, Gun House, to which surely ought to belong the cannon up-ended outside the old Police House next door to the New Inn, remains a link with the defence systems of the eighteenth and nineteenth centuries.

From New Romney to its member Lydd is about three miles as the crow flies, but considerably longer by the road which runs almost due north and south by Caldecot and Jack's Court, and enters Lydd by East Ripe and the railway station. The flat ridges of loose shingle of the Ripe, flecked with tufts and spreads of marram grass, represent a former coastline between Lydd and New Romney, and the geologically-minded tourist will be able to find sections through the sands and gravels showing the make-up of the lagoon and the subsequent tidal marsh which once rested behind the shelter of that coast. Away on the seaward skyline is the vast shingle promontory of Dungeness, the text-book example of an apposition beach for the geologists, shaped into its present form by the reaction of the opposing Channel and North Sea tides which meet at this point in the Strait of Dover. There is nothing else like it, except Chesil Bank. To the naturalist, the insect life and the uncommon flora, the succession of migrating birds, and the bird sanctuaries controlled by the Royal Society for the Protection of Birds are attractions enough. But there are also to be seen signal stations and a lighthouse, vast commercial workings for sand and gravel, more than a memory of " Operation Pluto," the undersea pipe-line of which here left Britain to supply petrol to our forces on the Continent, and as varied a collection of inhabited railway coaches and seaside bungalows as may be seen anywhere on the sea-edge of Britain. The landscape has a strange quality in winter: the dun-coloured shingle seems to hang fantastically in a skeleton framework of telegraph poles, and where sea and sky meet in a fore-shortened perspective, large ships sailing in a channel of deep water hug the land. It is a place to see.

The present-day interest of Lydd centres round its tree-girt church, the " Cathedral of the Marsh," which, although it was severely damaged during the recent war, still has in its embattled western tower a remarkable piece of Gothic architecture. This tower was very probably in building between 1435–50. It has a double western doorway with a finely proportioned four-light window above, all built as one graceful unit and framed within a deeply moulded continuous arch; within, the lower stage has a lofty lierne vault with moulded ribs and foliage-carved bosses. There is here no reflection of the influence of Lydd as a port,

or even of the standing of its wool-merchants whose wealth
was derived from the extensive inned lands of the Marsh, but
rather of the overlordship of the Archbishops of Canterbury,
whose power and architectural ambitions may be traced here
as well as at Hythe, Romney and Sandwich.

The history of Lydd which began in Saxon times can be well
documented from the reign of Edward I onwards. An extensive
series of its records is kept in the Town Hall. The port had
become blocked by shingle banks and part of its neighbouring
marsh reclaimed before the beginning of the fourteenth century.
Apart from the church, not a great deal of history is to be read
in its buildings, but the Court House in Cannon Street, and the
several homely Georgian houses of red brick can be set off
against the extensive military camps and the invention of the
high explosive called lyddite.

A schoolboy in Lydd told us an interesting version of local
history: the belfry at Brookland belonged really to Lydd
Church, from the tower of which it was removed by Cardinal
Wolsey when he was Rector. This alternative to the usually
accepted and slightly scandalous account of the origin of
Brookland's detached belfry is hard to beat as a curious piece of
misinformation. Thomas Wolsey held the vicarage of Lydd,
it seems from 1503 to 1514, as an absentee; it was not until 1515
that he was created a Cardinal. The story of the belfry can be
traced to a suggestion made at the Summer Meeting of the Kent
Archæological Society on Romney Marsh in 1879, when it was
thought that the predecessor of the Perpendicular tower of Lydd
Church " may have been a separate belfry of wood, resembling
that at Brookland." In such a way, and in seventy years, can a
local tradition grow.

Some three miles to the north-west lies Old Romney which,
until the choking of the harbour and the diversion of the Rother
from its site, seems to have flourished as a port. It was not, as
might be supposed from its present name, a township which
was in existence before the foundation of New Romney, for
that town itself, throughout the Middle Ages, had no prefix to
its name. Now it is but a very small and isolated hamlet surrounded by sheep pastures, little different perhaps from its

28   NEW ROMNEY : " St. John's Priory "

29   OLD ROMNEY : the church of St. Clement

30 THE MAGNIFICENT THIRTEENTH CENTURY CHANCEL OF ST. LEONARD'S CHURCH

31 CHURCH ROW, one of the steep hillside lanes

HYTHE

condition in 1377 when it housed but 133 inhabitants. The neat little Church of St. Clement (29) stands picturesquely in the meadows just north of the Rhee Wall; the interior, with its silver-grey woodwork, is an unspoiled piece of Queen Anne and Georgian taste. The sites of two medieval churches, St. Lawrence and St. Michael, are nearby, close to an ancient moat, while across the marsh, a mile away by the Ashford Road, are the gaunt ruins of Hope All Saints.

The non-corporate members of Romney included Dengemarsh and Oswaldstone. The former, which was inned and drained in the eighth century, lies to the south-east of Lydd, its name to-day indicating part of the shingle spread of Dungeness. Bromehill, another non-corporate member, lay on the border of Kent and Sussex. Its history was closely allied to that of Old Winchelsea, with which it had a common fate. On the authority of a nineteenth century Town Clerk of Lydd, it was in 1250 " a pretty little seaport town, much frequented. It had twenty-four taverns and was a member of the port of Romney." Could any town be more fortunate ?

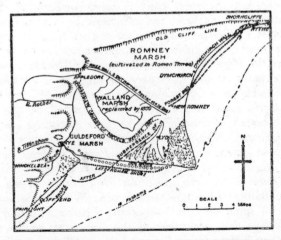

DEVELOPMENT OF THE COAST BETWEEN HYTHE AND HASTINGS

After W. V. Lewis

CHAPTER VI

HYTHE

HYTHE means a haven, yet Hythe has no haven; the hamlet of West Hythe, Hythe's sole member, likewise has no haven, being a couple of miles from the sea; the adjacent village of Lympne takes its name from the Limen, an earlier name of the River Rother, yet the Rother flows into the English Channel at Rye, fifteen miles away over the far side of Romney Marsh. How are these puzzling contradictions to be explained ? In general terms we can say that they are the result of the land-changes which have given rise to that still only half-explained mystery, Romney Marsh. Nennius, the ninth century author of *A Catalogue of British Wonders*, says: " The first marvel is the Limen [Romney] Marsh, for in it are 340 islands with men living on them. It is girt by 340 rocks, and in every rock is an eagle's nest, and 340 rivers flow into it; and there goes out of it into the sea but one river, which is called the Limen." Such a combination of wild fantasy and arithmetical exactness is worthy of the Rev. Professor Dodgson, but neither Nennius' explanation nor those of the geologists altogether resolve the mystery.

Before the Rhee Wall was constructed in Roman times, the Rother debouched into an estuary running below the hill from Lympne to Hythe, roughly along the line of the Military Canal. The seaward bank of the estuary was formed by the ever-growing barrier of shingle, year by year extending eastwards up the Channel. This estuary must have afforded the Romans a navigable haven, for Lympne was *Portus Lemanis* (*i.e.*, the port of the River Limen), comparable in importance with Reculver and Richborough, and like them the site of one of the fortresses built to defend the Saxon Shore. West Hythe remained a haven of some sort until about the fourteenth century, for Camden says that, according to the " memory of the great-grandfathers " West Hythe " was a harbour till the sea withdrew itself two centuries ago." The diversion of the course of the Rother deprived West Hythe haven of the river's scouring

32   ST. BARTHOLOMEW'S HOSPITAL : founded before 1276

33   THE ROYAL MILITARY CANAL, built in 1805–6 as a defence against invasion

HYTHE

34 YPRES TOWER from the Gungarden

35 LANDGATE, built *c.* 1340, is the N.E. entrance to the town

RYE

effect, but in any case the eastward shingle-drift and the silt brought down by the river were bound, in the course of centuries, to obstruct the haven. The western end of the estuary became unusable, and although for a time the Hythe end remained navigable, eventually the whole estuary became beach, marsh or firm land, so that in the latter half of the sixteenth century Camden reports that Hythe " can hardly maintain the name [of port] against the heaps of sand which shut out the sea for a great way." By the end of Elizabeth's reign its day as a port was over.

The old town of Hythe lies stretched out east and west along the steep hillside overlooking the site of the former haven. Its narrow main streets, like parallel terraces cut out along the contours of the slope, are joined by even narrower lanes (31), shut in by high garden walls, that run so steeply uphill that one of them, Church Hill, has had to be stepped. No map or plan can do justice to Hythe; its situation on the hillside gives it a three-dimensional quality that demands an elevation or an isometric view as well as a plan for a proper understanding of the disposition of its streets and alleys, walks and water-ways, houses, church and shops. It seems safe to assume that the general layout of the older part of the town has remained unchanged throughout the centuries of Hythe's existence. Elsewhere, the School of Musketry, with its attendant buildings, belongs to the early part of the nineteenth century, and the suburb which lies between the Military Canal and the sea is still more recent.

Domesday Book refers to Hythe merely to note that 225 burgesses in the borough belong to the manor of Saltwood. Saltwood, a village at the crest of the hill, above Hythe, had been granted to Christchurch, Canterbury, by Canute, and it remained in the hands of the Archbishop until Cranmer surrendered it to Henry VIII in 1541. As lord of the manor, the Archbishop was able to supervise the government of Hythe, and he appointed the bailiff of the town. Cranmer granted the town a lease of the appointment for ninety-nine years, but the lease was defeated soon afterwards by the surrender of the manor to the Crown, and the townspeople had to wait until

1575, when Queen Elizabeth granted them a new charter, before they acquired the right of electing their chief officer, henceforward known as the Mayor. In St. Leonard's Church a brass commemorates John Bredgman, *obit* 1581, Hythe's last bailiff and first mayor, who was instrumental in securing the charter of 1575.

Not only in secular, but also in ecclesiastical, affairs Hythe was appendant to Saltwood. The Church of St. Leonard was a chapel attached to the rectory of Saltwood, and remained so until 1844, when it became a separate vicarage. The church is built high up the hillside, on a natural plateau which, as we shall presently notice, was so small as to create serious problems when a later generation wanted to enlarge the building.

The nave, though much altered, is late Norman. The arch at the east end of the south aisle and the elaborate external doorway in the west wall of the north transept plainly date this part of the church to the latter half of the twelfth century. The Norman chancel was transformed, during the thirteenth century, into the Early English masterpiece which caused Francis Bond to describe it as " the finest chancel of any parish church of its size in England, not to say in Europe " (30). The floor of the chancel is raised 4 feet above the floor of the nave, and the sanctuary is 18 inches above the level of the chancel. A noble flight of nine broad steps leads from the nave to the chancel. The columns supporting the high roof of the chancel are richly decorated, and the whole effect of soaring splendour is strongly reminiscent of Canterbury Cathedral. Part of the design for the rebuilding of the chancel had to wait 600 years before it was carried out, for the vaulted stone roof was not built until the first part of the nineteenth century.

In raising the chancel above the level of the nave the Early English architect made the most, æsthetically, of a plan which was forced upon him by liturgical requirements. The processional circumambulation of the church was an essential part of the medieval liturgy. At Hythe the architect found himself in difficulty because of the size of the little terrace on which the church stands. If he extended the chancel eastward, as he wanted to do, up to the public road which forms the eastern boundary of the churchyard, it would not leave room for the procession to pass round the east end of the building and yet remain on consecrated ground. Therefore, beneath the chancel, he built a vaulted passage leading from south to north, so that the procession instead of passing round the outside of the chancel passed underneath it. Later, when the south porch, which extends to the road, was built side-doors were cut in the east and west walls so that the processional way was not closed up.

Apart from its architectural interest, the ambulatory (or "crypt" as it is usually called) attracts visitors, at 6d. each, because of the quantity of human remains deposited there. The well-ordered rows of hundreds of skulls, grinning together in neighbourly derision at the staring strangers, and the neatly-piled thigh-bones, computed to represent upwards of 4,000 men, women and children, have proved a source of morbid fascination for many generations of townspeople and visitors, who have evolved a variety of theories to account for their presence. They have usually been thought to be the bones of those slain in battle—as for whom, and which battle, there are numerous possibilities to choose from; one of the most popular and, romantically most engaging, theories is that these bones represent the mortal remains of the Britons who fell in a battle waged against the invading Saxons on the seashore, the bones of the Saxons finding a corresponding resting place beneath the Church of St. Mary and St. Eanswythe at Folkestone. In fact, they are of more prosaic origin. The medieval churchyard was small, and new burials constantly disinterred old ones. The bones thus unearthed were placed in the ambulatory, which may have been taken into use as a charnel-house even before the practice of liturgical processions came to an end. Similar, although smaller deposits of bones have been discovered beneath other churches, as, for instance, in Kent at Upchurch and the former Church of St. Peter at Dover, and there is nothing inherently improbable in the legend of a hoard of human bones under the parish church at Folkestone. Some few of the Hythe skulls are pierced, a fact sufficient to account for the battle theory, but in truth they were victims of no more martial a weapon than the sexton's spade.

In the south transept of the church (rebuilt in 1751 by the Deedes family, who owned the fine mellow red-brick house just below the church in Hillside Street) is a painted iron chest in which the registers are kept. By repute it came out of the Armada; it is of Netherlands workmanship. Two years before the south transept was rebuilt, the tower, which collapsed in 1739, was re-erected. The earthquake of 1580, which caused the cliffs and castle walls at Dover to collapse, set the Hythe bells ringing; did it, perhaps, weaken the tower, contributing to its downfall 160 years later ? In the vestry on the ground floor of the tower is a memorial tablet to Thomas Spratt (*obit* 1619), who was thrice Mayor and Bailiff to Yarmouth, and who was " of those that did carry the canopie over the Kinge at his cronation "—a timely reminder that our present interest is in Hythe as a Cinque Port.

The room over the fourteenth century porch served as the Town Council meeting-place until the Town Hall in High Street was built—or reconstructed out of some earlier building—in 1794 (37). Until recently some municipal documents were still kept in the parvise, though latterly with more care than a hundred years ago, when the visitor could handle the records and carry off one or two as souvenirs if he were sufficiently interested. The town records are of the greatest importance for the history of the Cinque Ports, and they have survived centuries of casual neglect with less damage than could be expected or hoped for. Now they are treated with a respect proper to their importance. They are housed at the small well-arranged museum at the Public Library (Oaklands, Stade Street) and many of them are on exhibition. For example, amongst other things the visitor can see a deed of Henry Chichele, Archbishop of Canterbury, appointing William Buris as Bailiff in 1441; there is an agreement made between the Cinque Ports at a Brotherhood in 1392 settling how dues payable to the Crown should be apportioned between the Ports, and providing that any Port should have the right of requiring a Brotherhood to be summoned; there are reproductions of Edward I's Charter of 1278 to the Cinque Ports and of Elizabeth's Charter of 1575 to Hythe; and there is an

36   PEACOCK'S SCHOOL, a brick building of 1636

RYE

37   THE TOWN HALL, 1794, with the covered
market below

HYTHE

97

38 THE EAST END

39 One of the oldest
working clocks in
England : it was
made in 1560 at
Winchelsea

"For our time is a
very shadow that
passeth away."

ST. MARY, RYE
THE CATHEDRAL OF EAST SUSSEX

agreement between Dover and Hythe, dated March 15th, 1588, about their respective shares of the cost of providing a ship of eight-score tons, the *Vineyard* of London, against the "pretended Spanyshe invasion."

Hythe's earliest ship-service had been for five ships, but in the 1335 survey of the potential strength of the Ports, Hythe was reported to have three vessels, of 120, 100 and 80 tons, compared with a total tonnage of 650 at Sandwich, 340 at Dover, 320 at Romney and no less than 1680 at Rye and Winchelsea. Six years later the King threatened to annul the liberties of Hythe and Romney unless they performed their service with five ships apiece, but the Warden was constrained to reply that there was no suitable ship at Hythe and only one at Romney. This return is difficult to understand, because for the Siege of Calais in 1345 Hythe provided six ships, and they must have been of moderate size, for their complement was 112 men. In 1378 there is a record of a town-ship, owned by the borough and employed in the fishing industry, but in 1428 Hythe had to hire a ship from Smallhythe to perform its ship-service. In 1566, before the haven had finally become useless, Hythe possessed the modest fleet of four vessels of 60 tons, three of 30 tons, and twenty-five fishing boats with 160 fishermen, but, significantly, by 1625 it had nothing but fishing boats.

Hythe never shared the prosperity of other Ports such as Sandwich, Rye and Winchelsea. It was not only the eastward shingle-drift and the turning of the Rother away from Hythe haven that caused its decline. The French raids left their mark, and in other ways, too, misfortune came upon the town. On May 3rd, 1400, fire consumed 200 houses (surely the greater part of the town, for even in Elizabeth's reign the larger towns of Faversham and Dover had less than 400 houses each), and about the same time five ships were lost at sea, with a hundred Hythe men.

We may be thankful that the portsmen were induced by Henry IV not to desert their ill-starred town, as they proposed, for we, thereby, "should have lost a gesture and a pose." Present-day Hythe bears no outward and visible sign of its past infelicities. Its varied but congruous old-fashioned streets, its mellow and pleasant buildings, its fourteenth century stone-built hospitals of St. Bartholomew (32) and St. John, the latter, in High Street, now undergoing repair, its small and neat Georgian Town Hall (37) (prudently connected by a private door to its neighbour, of good repute, the " White Hart," which recently celebrated its 300th anniversary as a house of rest and refreshment), its Ladies' Walk, planted with wych elms to commemorate the jubilee of George III, and its fine elm-avenue beside the Royal Military Canal, all give an impression of prosperity and peace.

But peaceful though it now seems, the Canal (33) was constructed in a time of war and desperate national danger, when Napoleon's forces lay for months at Boulogne waiting for the favourable opportunity, that never came, to cross the Channel and invade the shores of Kent and Sussex. Romney Marsh was regarded as a likely landing-place, and to isolate it from the mainland the Canal, twenty-seven miles in length, was cut along the foot of the old cliff, from Hythe to Winchelsea. Every third of a mile the straight line of the Canal makes a break, so as to enable a battery placed in an embrasure at each kink in the north bank to enfilade the adjacent stretch of water. This was by no means the only line of defence. As in 1940, there were schemes for flooding the Marsh (it could be done in the space of two tides) to hold up the enemy, and along the coast were built the string of block-houses, known as Martello Towers, a characteristic feature of the south-east coastal scene. The Home Guard of the late war were probably less contemptuous of the defensive value of Martello Towers than the military pundits of the latter part of the nineteenth century, who dismissed them as being out of date and useless. The defence of Hythe against the threatened Napoleonic invasion was further strengthened by three forts built on the shore— Twiss Fort, where the Imperial Hotel stands, Sutherland Fort, now a ruin beyond the rifle-range, and Moncrief Fort, farther to the west.

Hythe's only limb was West Hythe, now a hamlet two miles west of Hythe, on the north side of the Military Canal. There is little to be said about it, either by way of history or of descrip-

40 WATCHBELL STREET

41 THE HOSPITAL, MERMAID STREET

THE COBBLED STREETS OF RYE

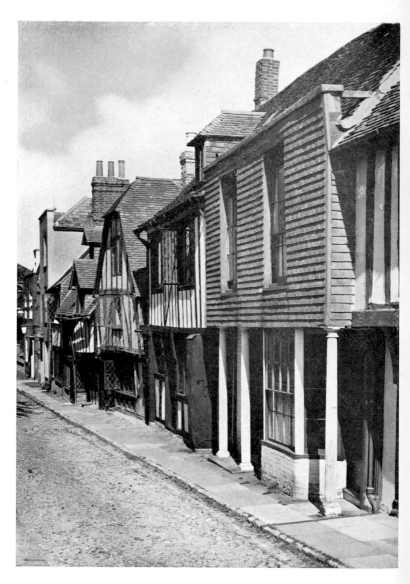

42   CHURCH SQUARE, RYE

tion. Since the time whereof the memory of men runneth not to the contrary, it has not been a place of any consequence. It is not named in Domesday Book, an omission that suggests that even then it was of no great moment. In a return of 1564 we read " the sum of all there is in this parish, four households, 14 communicants, six unable." It had a chapel, dedicated to Our Lady of West Hythe, but it seems already to have been ruinous when the roof was burnt out sometime between 1615 and 1620, and a ruin it remains.

Half a mile west of Hythe the ruins of the Roman fortress are strewn down the steep hillside. Their disjected state is due to an ancient landslip which was so violent as in some places to overturn the 14-foot thick walls and throw them out of their original line. It is impossible now to trace the original plan of the castle, although excavations in 1850, as contemporary illustrations show, uncovered massive and undisturbed masonry walls and piers below ground level. The excavations had to be filled in, because sheep persisted in falling into them, and the incoherent visible remains of Stutfall make it hard to believe that once it was a base of the *Classis Britannica* and one in the great series of defensive links, which included the fortresses of Richborough and Pevensey. But so it was, just as the Canal immediately below it was part of the defences against the Napoleonic invasion threat, and the mechanical ears that adorn— or did during the war—the brow of the hill above were part of the defences against the even greater menace of 1940. Methods of defence change with the centuries; in this corner of England the fact and need of defence remain unchanging.

NOTE. Several pieces of ornamental silver made from coronation canopy furnishings are briefly mentioned in this book, but there is none finer than a scoll-handled tankard marked for the year 1661 in the collection of the Goldsmith's company. It is inscribed " This Pott was made of ye Silver of ye Canopie when Kinge Charles ye 2^d was crownd, Aprill 23^d 1661 ", and engraved with the arms of Paramour impaling Cleve, and of Boys and Littledale. Tobias Cleve was one of the Sandwich barons at the coronation ; he died in 1671 and his grand-daughter married a Paramour of Fordwich. The other arms belong to the middle years of the eighteenth century. This notable tankard was exhibited with the Historic Plate of the City of London at Goldsmiths' Hall in 1951.

CHAPTER VII

THE TWO ANCIENT TOWNS

WINCHELSEA

IT is curious to think that the old-world buildings of the present Winchelsea are in fact those of a new town (44). The original town of Winchelsea, one of the most active ports on the south-east coast, has been entirely engulfed by the sea. Its site is roughly indicated by the existing parish of St. Thomas-the-Apostle which, strangely enough, lies on the eastern bank of the River Rother, opposite Rye Harbour. On its peninsula it had communication by land only to the west; on all points but this it faced a great expanse of water.

Old Winchelsea may have been in existence in pre-Conquest or even in Roman times. It was probably regarded by William I as belonging to the Cinque Ports Confederation; by 1200, at any rate, in company with Rye, it was looked upon as providing ship-service with Hastings. The town's short-lived prosperity reached its peak in the early part of the thirteenth century, when it was the anchorage and assembly point of the naval forces used against France.

In the first part of the thirteenth century, several storms of quite exceptional severity, accompanied by high tides and by the inundation of the south-east coast, had struck the old town. No doubt the gradual wasting of the clay headland of Fairlight to the westward deprived this piece of coast of protection and was thus a factor in its destruction. In 1250, according to Holinshed, " besides other hurt that was done in bridges, mills, breaks, and banks, there were 300 houses and some churches drowned with the high rising of the water course." Mathew Paris, possibly himself a Winchelsea man, gives a circumstantial account of the great damage done to the town in storms of 1252.

The next misfortune, and one from which the town never recovered, was the punitive visitation in 1266 of Prince Edward. In 1288 came the end. A great storm, with the most violent wind and high tides, broke over the coast. The land had been

43   THE QUAY AT RYE

44   TYPICAL TILE-HUNG COTTAGES AT WINCHELSEA

45   From the South

46   THE ARMS OF THE CINQUE PORTS over the West Porch

WINCHELSEA : CHURCH OF ST. THOMAS OF CANTERBURY

slowly sinking at least since the eighth century. With the impetus of the storm the sea breached the sea-walls, and from Appledore to Old Winchelsea, south and west, the land was drowned. The River Rother forsook its course and made a new outfall by Rye. The town of Old Winchelsea already, as Leland says, " a very soore and manifest ruine, be reason of olde rages of the se," was completely destroyed. Since that time the sandhills and shingle of Camber, built up against the promontory of Dungeness, have obliterated its very site.

It was by the direct interest of Edward I that arrangements were made in 1280 for the setting out and building of a new town, for it was then evidently clear that the old town was in no condition to be restored or rebuilt. The new foundation was on a prominent hill, called Iham, at the eastern end of the Guestling-Icklesham ridge; it had good landward communication, while eastward lay The Camber (*La Chambre*), a convenient harbour with access to the Channel. For its purpose, the geographical situation with control of the Normandy crossing seemed all that could be desired. To encourage settlement here, the King commissioned the Lord Warden of the Cinque Ports to lay out the site of the new town and granted almost all of it to " the barons of the port and town of Winchelsea," confirming them in the privileges and franchises they had previously enjoyed at Old Winchelsea. For nearly a century it enjoyed great pros-perity, and bade fair to rival the record of the old town as one of the principal southern ports for continental trade. Its export trade, which was extensive, was in grain and wool. In ship-service it normally provided the largest number of ships from the Western Ports, and in Edward I's opening war with France, the largest number of any.

The new town consisted of some ninety acres which were to be regularly laid out in thirty-nine quarters divided by eight streets intersecting to all intents at right angles. Such " chess-board " plans were a feature of the bastides of southern France built between the eleventh and the thirteenth centuries. Edward had done much to encourage the economic life of those in Gascony, and it is not surprising that as King he was mindful of the English trade in Gascon wines when he interested himself

K*

in the foundation of New Winchelsea. The regular plan can still be seen in North Street, Mill Road, High Street, Back Lane, German Street, Higham Green, St. Thomas's Street, Castle Street, Rectory Lane and Robert's Hill, the chief streets at the north-east part of the town where most of the buildings which still remain are situated. But many of the blocks are now pastures, and much of the site, though it was marked out, was never in fact occupied, the delightfully spacious present-day village being therefore an arrested development. A complete contemporary record gives the streets and holdings as they were laid out, and the names of the first owners.

The defences are noteworthy. On the east and overlooking the roadstead the steep natural cliff made a major artificial defence unnecessary, though the cliff top, it appears, was strengthened by a mud parapet with embrasures. Elsewhere the town was given to some extent the protection of a wall, which has all but disappeared, and in 1321 it was enclosed by a deep and narrow ditch, a sector of which can still be seen in the meadow close to the southern entrance at the now isolated New Gate. The picturesque fourteenth century Strand Gate (48), made well known to artists by its inclusion in Turner's *Liber Studiorum*, has four drum towers and two portcullis arches, and is now open to the sky. It led by the steep Strand Hill to the quay-side, and from its archway is a striking view across the Royal Military Canal and the flats of the River Brede, the site of the former roadstead, to the grey and red-roofed town of Rye. Its strategic position was again recognised in the anxious days of 1940 when it became a strong-point.

The Land or Pipewell Gate on the north commanded the almost equally steep descent to the ferry over the Brede. The present gateway bears on its outer (western) face a much-worn coat of arms and a name above it, scarcely to be read, as I. Helde; John Helde was Mayor of Winchelsea in 1404–05, at which time the structure was repaired. The gateway is now roofless, and its stairway blocked. Though the town walls have fallen, except for one piece near Pipewell Gate, it is not difficult to trace the area which they bounded, and in exceptionally dry or frosty weather to see in the meadows the outline of some long-forgotten quarter. The clues are there, and it needs only a mild sense of detection.

Near the centre of the town, and occupying the whole of one important quarter, is the Church of St. Thomas of Canterbury (45), a fine piece of Decorated architecture enriched with graceful mouldings and delicate carving. The building as it now appears is not in its original and imposing form; it was planned as a large church with a chancel having north and south chapels, a central tower, and an aisled nave with transepts. The present nave is the original chancel, the arch of which has been filled in and fitted with a sixteenth century porch; the former nave transepts lie in ruins, and of the original nave, which possibly had two western towers, nothing is to be seen. There is a theory that the nave may have been destroyed during one of the several French raids upon the town. It seems more likely, however, that the town had declined in its prosperity before the nave had been completed beyond its foundations, but on the evidence of a fifteenth century doorway in the south transept, that transept seems to have been in use. Apart from the porch and certain obvious modern restorations, the whole church dates from about 1320, that is, from some forty-five years after the foundation of the town. The bold outline and simple coherent plan are set off by the rich and elaborate " Kentish " tracery of its windows within their arcades of Sussex marble, while the presence of original fittings, carefully restored, adds much to its interest. The piscina and sedilia on the south side of the sanctuary with their cinquefoiled heads and crocketed gables designed as a single architectural group, and the charming little parapet of the sanctuary with its delicate tracery, are as good an example of period taste as will be found anywhere in a parish church. It is tempting to think that it was the work of a master-mason, commissioned by the King himself, whose designs elsewhere had received royal approbation.

The immediate connection of the church with the Cinque Ports begins appropriately enough at the entrance, with the arms of the Ports, *England dimidiating Azure three hulls of ships or*, on a much-weathered shield of soft yellow sandstone which occupies the middle niche in the gable above the frame of the door (46).

Then there are tombs of the Alard family, wealthy traders whose fortunes were largely bound up with the Gascon wine-trade. Gervase Alard was in 1300 Captain and Admiral of the Western Fleet, and a little later Mayor of Winchelsea. His grandson, Stephen, was Admiral some twenty-four years later, and it is characteristic of the traditional callings of the men of Winchelsea that at much the same time as the Alards held these royal offices they were widely engaged in the lucrative practices of piracy and ship-wrecking. Stephen endowed a chantry in the Chapel of St. Nicholas here in his parish church, and in the present south chapel are his family tombs (47). That on the east, a magnificent recessed tomb with a richly carved arch, crocketed gable and background of diaper work, has a cross-legged effigy of a man in complete mail with surcoat, holding a heart in his hands. Traditionally he is Gervase Alard, and the architectural and costume details would certainly support a date of about 1310 for the effigy. The heads of Edward I and his second wife, Margaret, the young sister of the King of France, here depicted with a countenance most dolorous, are outstanding features of the monument. This tomb formed the setting for " Safe from the Battle's Din ", one of Sir John Everett Millais' sweetly-pretty pictures of children. Nearby, to the west, is a plain arched tomb-recess with a canopied niche on each side which may have been for Sir Stephen Alard himself, though more probably it belonged to the family of Oxenbridge of Brede, whose arms it bears. At any rate, it is of the period 1325–30, and there is no denying the beauty of the exquisite work in Caen stone. About the third Alard tomb there is no doubt: a legend in Lombardic capitals round a stone in the floor indented for a floriate cross promises fifty days pardon to him who shall pray for the soul of Reynaud Alard who died in 1354.

There is a striking memorial to the men of the Cinque Ports who were engaged in the Great European War. Three windows in the north aisle (among others) have been filled with modern glass painted by Douglas Strachan, vivid in its intense blue and scraps of scarlet, ambitious in its design, but with its odd grace a fitting tribute to the lawless portsmen who could also praise

47   ST. THOMAS OF CANTERBURY : the Farnecombe Chantry (North Chapel)

48   THE STRAND GATE still spans the road to Rye

WINCHELSEA

49 " ST. ANTHONY OF PADUA " : a fifteenth century house
recently renovated

50 THE MERMAID INN : a restored fifteenth century building

RYE

their God. A nearby altar of blue Hornton stone relieved in silver provides an authentic medieval touch.

Winchelsea is quiet and leisurely in its air—" a town in a trance," says Coventry Patmore in his song of the Sussex Marshes, " a sunny dream of centuries ago." The white painted weatherboard of its well-kept houses (51), the much-restored fourteenth century Court Hall, a stone building with a museum above and the Water Bailiff's prison below, the impressive chancel of a Franciscan convent church, all set against a wide background of grass and trees, make this a place of visual delight. A bold red and blue poster in the church square which says that Mr. Gregory Peck is to be seen in *Twelve O'Clock High* at the cinema in a neighbouring town is, on this brilliant evening in May, an untimely reminder of the twentieth century; the more so, perhaps, as it stands blocking the entrance to a medieval cellar, one of the " vast caves and vaults " of Evelyn's *Diary*, which were intended for the use of the wine-traders. The maritime interests of Winchelsea are forgotten, apart from the daily watch still kept between seven and eight in the morning by the Keeper of the Look-out, who receives an annual fee of £1 2s. 6d. for his services. A frock coat, top hat and large telescope seem to be the accepted uniform for this officer, who still watches for the ships from France.

The military history of Winchelsea is largely the history of successive incursions by the French. But off Winchelsea, in 1350, the English fleet, commanded by Edward III in company with his twenty-year-old son, Edward the Black Prince, joined battle with the Spaniards who were returning home down channel after the war in Flanders. Froissart's graphic account has ensured that the memory of this naval battle will never fail. In 1360 and again in 1380 the French wrought great havoc. The slaughter in the former year is traditionally perpetuated in Deadman's Lane, an old name for the present Hogtrough Lane; and the damage in 1380 was very severe, both to the church and to the town defences. The Black Death here, as elsewhere, took its toll and added to the desolation of the scene. In an official return in 1366 the bailiff of the town recorded no less than 385 tenements as waste, burnt and uninhabited.

By the middle years of the sixteenth century this unstable coastline saw yet further changes, and the famous harbour of Winchelsea was in decay. The accumulation of silt and the dumping of ship's ballast to give more room for cargo gradually filled even its deepest channels, and as Winchelsea declined, so Rye grew and gradually absorbed the trade of its neighbour. The one event of the century was Queen Elizabeth's visit in 1573; the efforts to entertain her were brave, but the royal description of the town as " Little London " was perhaps more cynical than polite. After this royal visit, a modern historian reminds us, the town went to sleep again for a couple of centuries; it lacked staple industry and its life blood ebbed. Houses and whole streets became gardens and pleasant meadows. In 1587, it is officially recorded, there were no ships, captains or mariners, but only one sailor whose name, William Bucston, has thus been preserved down the years.

One last note about Winchelsea. If you drink from St. Leonard's Well—it is in the meadows underneath the north-western hillside just beyond the windmill (52), fenced with barbed wire and its noisome water almost covered by watercress and overhanging brambles—your heart, according to a local legend, remains here and hither you will in the end return.

RYE

The Ancient Town of Rye has become one of the tourist centres of Sussex. Its several pebble-cobbled, grass-grown, crooked and irregular streets with their picturesque tile-hung, weatherboarded and timber-framed houses are the particular delight of artists (40, 42), and for the antiquary there are the architectural problems of the fine church, the many obviously old houses, and others in which a Georgian front masks a much older structure. There is a modern side, but on the hill all is discreet; the pawnbroker almost apologises for the diminutive symbols of his calling, placed high up on the side wall of East

51   THE DIGNIFIED HOUSES OF CHURCH SQUARE, WINCHELSEA

52   THE DISUSED WINDMILL overlooking the Brede Valley, Winchelsea

Street and not in the main road. In the words of an old fisher-
man drowsing away an afternoon on Town Salts, accompanied
by an expressive over-the-shoulder jerk with his thumb, " They
up there ain't we down here," and the atmosphere of the Quay
(43) and the Strand is certainly different from that of the
superior Mermaid and Watchbell Streets.

The time to see Rye is in the early morning when the Olde
Tea Shoppes and the knick-knack counters are not yet in
business. The enterprising Corporation has provided accurate
and readable notices on all the places of historic interest; a
coloured panoramic map of the town is exhibited at several
points, and there are even helpful directions to a view-point,
Hilder's Cliff, which has a magnificent shadowless landscape of
Romney Marsh.

This strange landscape with its oneness of land and sky and
sea is perhaps best seen from the church tower (up which a
courteous verger will take you at a small charge), or at last light
from the parapet of the old battery called the Gungarden. It
has that sentiment in landscape, wrote Basil Champneys, an
architect who lived at Winchelsea and knew it well, that " pro-
ceeds neither from grandeur of scale nor ruggedness of outline
nor from a vivid clearness in atmosphere nor from any special
or exotic conditions whatever, but grows up in the simplicity
and harmony of native scenes, and demands no energy and no
effort, but only a little sympathy."

A fitting introduction to Rye of Cinque Port fame stands in
the road from Winchelsea, a stone shield bearing the arms of
the Ports which was removed from the Strand Gate at its final
destruction in 1820, and reset in the Strand frontage of the last
house at the foot of Mermaid Street.

Rye and Winchelsea were attached to Hastings as their Head
Port before 1190, but during the thirteenth century they were
themselves given the constitutional standing of Head Ports and
denominated the Two Ancient Towns. Rye, like Winchelsea,
until 1247 came under overlordship of the Abbey of Fécamp.
The two Ancient Towns found in alternate years one Bailiff
for the Yarmouth herring fishing, and as late as the fourteenth
century Rye was receiving rents from Yarmouth. Winchelsea,

it will be remembered, was called upon to find twice the number of ships, but later on with the decay of that town, the affairs of Rye prospered. The Cinque Ports history of Rye is long and well documented; the many interesting records kept in the basement of the Town Hall are properly calendared and are available to accredited students on proper application.

Here are one or two items from its very full history. In 1300, Rye supplied three ships, *Snake*, *Rose* and *Godyere*, each with two constables and thirty-nine hands, for service in the war against Scotland. As an example of the Ryers' "peaceful" activities, there is William Longe, the town's burgess in the Parliament of 1410, whose duty it was to maintain an anti-piracy patrol in the Channel. So well did he perform his duty that he found no scruple of conscience in himself seizing a Florentine carrack loaded with Rochelle wine, which he took into a west country port. In spite of an immediate order for his arrest, he sailed again for sea. His next escapade was to take eleven Flemish wine ships bound from Rochelle and to lead them, with their crews, into Rye. It seems that he was apprehended at sea by the Admiral of the Cinque Ports Fleet acting on the King's instructions; at any rate, after eighteen months in the Tower of London he was pardoned, and so well did his fellow-Ryers think of him that after this, between 1412 and 1422, he represented them in four successive Parliaments. At the end of their effective life the Rye contingent in the fleet against the Armada earned the Queen's approbation, and she presented the town with half a dozen "brass guns" bearing the Royal Arms of Spain.

The town was first walled and its gates built probably in the reign of Edward III against the French. The sea has washed away much of the eastern side of the town; its former extent seaward can be estimated by an imaginary reconstruction of the line of the town wall between the still existing Land Gate on the north and the Ypres Tower on the south-east. It was completely sacked by the French in 1339, and visited again in 1377, 1385 and 1448, with dire results to the inhabitants and their buildings. In the 1377 raid, the French removed even the church bells, but they were recovered by the Rye men who made a special expedition to France for that purpose only two years later.

In the sixteenth century, especially after the decline of the once-important Winchelsea, it became well known for its extensive fishing industry and as crossing-place to France. It twice provided a refuge for bands of Huguenots from France, who settled here industriously with their weaving trade; a pewter flagon with a later inscription describing its use " at the Celebration of the Lord's Supper by the Minister of the Protestant Refugees who found an Asylum in Rye after the Revocation of the Edict of Nantes, 22nd October, 1685," a relic of their stay, may be seen in a case in the church. The retreat of the sea in the reign of Elizabeth completed one phase in the history of Rye. Beginning as a small hill surrounded by tidal water (it took its name from the Old English *æt thære iege*, " at the island," the final r of the definite article becoming wrongly attached to the noun to make *atte Rie*) it became a peninsula. By the early part of the seventeenth century Rye Harbour was in decay, but the maritime industries of fishing and boat-building saved the town from utter ruin. Fishing does still continue and there are usually one or two small smacks tied up at the Quay, but the picturesque Rye barge with its lug-sail and out-of-size rudder, the fishing dandies for the northern ports, and the Rye Bay trawlers, are now but memories of a once flourishing industry based on the ready supply of Sussex oak. Probably its last naval building was mortar-boats for the Crimean war.

There is more than a tenuous link with the old seafaring and sea-roving memories of Rye in the celebrations of the Fifth of November, as anyone who has seen the annual torchlight procession, with its ritual end of the burning of the boat on the Town Salts, will agree. The shadows of flames on the Ypres Tower and the upward swirling eddies of black smoke awake far-off memories of the horror of the French raids.

The sturdy independence of the Cinque Port sailors was passed down from generation to generation in this quiet seaboard town which had a more than usual distrust of " foreigners " and strangers. For about a century from 1715, most of its mayors came from four closely related families; even amongst Rotten Boroughs it was a notoriously bad one. It is not surprising that in the eighteenth century the men of Rye were expert and courageous practitioners in the smuggling of spirits and wool, the town itself with its convenient situation and many stone-vaulted medieval storage cellars becoming a headquarters for the famous gangs of Romney Marsh. The exploits of Dr. Syn and the ballad of Will Watch the Bold Smuggler present well enough the romantic story. John Wesley, when he preached in Sussex in 1773, found "abundance of people willing to hear the good word, at Rye in particular . . . but they will not part from the accursed thing, smuggling . . .", and Wesley feared that his labour with the Ryers would be in vain. By all accounts it was.

Of the fourteenth century town walls there remain considerable stretches behind the houses on the south side of Cinque Ports Street, the most complete section being opposite the Regent Cinema. The Landgate (35), which secured the northern approach, is a picturesque feature of mellow sandstone rubble and local ironstone, and with its machicolations, portcullis grooves, two hinge-hooks for the sturdy timber doors of the inner arch, and *meutrières*, it should satisfy the most exacting of sightseers. Overlooking Rye Harbour is Ypres Tower (34), a heavy square structure of three stories with three-quarter round towers at its angles. It was long used as a prison, and there are prisoners' scribblings in one of the turrets and a shackling ring in the floor. There is some reason for thinking that the tower had already been in existence since the middle of the thirteenth century when the town wall was laid out, but its name is derived from one John Yprys, who purchased the property in 1430 from the Corporation. Nearby, on the town wall adjoining the old prison-yard, a battlement has been exposed by bomb damage.

The top of the hill which is Rye is crowned by what is often known as the Cathedral of East Sussex, the parish church of St. Mary Virgin (38). Roof above roof, with red brick and tile predominant, the town rises upon its hill from the surrounding levels, and the squat embattled church tower, with its low spire giving the constant impression of a ship brought up against the weather, is one of the landmarks of this seaboard corner of England. It is likewise a memorial to the piety and industry of the people of Rye, who rebuilt and added to their church after the various destructions by the French, the stains of whose fires are still to be seen in the older Norman parts of the fabric. The Reformation did not leave this noble church unscathed, and the late nineteenth century saw a drastic restoration, in the worst possible Victorian taste. Its fortune in the recent war was more kind, and apart from some of the windows, happily it remained undamaged. It is a church of memorable features: the clerestory passage in the walls of the south chapel, nave and transepts, which in its original form must have been copied from that at Fécamp; the two Norman reliquaries in the east wall of the chancel; an exquisite carved table now used as an altar, which Herbert Cescinsky has described as almost the finest example of mahogany furniture in England to-day; one or two pieces of unusually fine furniture in the south transept, gifts of the faithful; a window designed by Burne-Jones and made by the Company of æsthetic adventurers in the last year of William Morris's life; and over all the great clock made in 1560 by a man of Winchelsea, its pendulum swinging free in the church and its quarter-boys, delightful cherubs of the eighteenth century, striking their chime on gilded bells (39).

The former Flushing Inn in Market Street contains an interesting tapestry-like wall-painting, with fantastic birds and beasts, including an elephant, in a dense dark-green foliage. Jane Seymour's coat in a shield of Royal Arms (which can be dated, very conveniently, to 1536–37), a triple inscription in Latin, " To God alone Honour and [Glory]," and the Magnificat in black letter, all add to its atmosphere of craftsmanship for its own sake. Under the Flushing Inn, with an entrance from the street, is a vaulted cellar which traditionally was a store den for contraband Hollands.

The streets still paved with kidney-stone cobbles are Conduit, Mermaid (41) and Watchbell (40), and each has notable buildings. The Augustine Friary on the steep hillside of Conduit Street has been spoiled by utilitarian additions and is now a church house, auction-room and public hall. An inserted floor cuts and blocks the fine Decorated windows, the leaf-tracery of which is to be seen only from a private garden. In Mermaid Street is the restored fifteenth century Mermaid Inn (50), now forlorn and empty, but still a favourite with the water-colour painter. Nearby is the old Hospital (41), a fine three-gabled timber-framed house in which medieval features are covered by Tudor and good modern additions. It was once the house of Samuel Jeake the Younger, the son of the elder Samuel, hop- and wool-merchant and Town Clerk of Rye, who compiled in 1678 *Charters of the Cinque Ports, Two Ancient Towns and their Members*, the first history of the Ports and one that will remain a standard work. The younger Jeake built the house nearly opposite as a store, first, as a good astrologer like his father, making sure that the occasion was propitious; in the wall is a stone recording the date, June 13th, 1689, and the characters of the horoscope.

Watchbell Street (40), with its picturesque brick and tile-hung gables and dignified seventeenth century plaster fronts, is so named from the alarm bell which gave warning of French raids. In the last twenty years there has been much scraping of timber-framing and judicious restoration; the result, at its best, can be seen in St. Anthony (49), a fifteenth century house with a finely moulded bressumer which less than a quarter of a century ago was in ruins. Of more than passing interest is Peacock's Grammar School in the High Street (36), a Caroline building with a striking pilastered façade of red brick. Its rigid and formal design, although it exhibits an odd sense of proportion, obviously owes a good deal to the Renaissance, and at the same time incorporates details from a Gothic background. Who, we wonder, was the architect of this school-house built in 1636 in a style so far removed from that of the usual domestic fashion of Rye? It was a fitting school for Denis Duval, the main character of Thackeray's last work of fiction; now it is the Rye Workmens' Conservative Club.

The George Inn, on the opposite side of the street, has a delightful white-and-gold assembly room (now used as a dining-room) with a minstrels' gallery. The small Town Hall of 1742 formerly had a market in the arcade below. It houses many things of interest: the town pillory, which is still in working order; gibbet-chains, with the actual remains of John Breeds, whose story is well known in Rye and recorded on a grave-slab in the church; and a series of records of great value in any study of the history of the Cinque Ports. Of special interest are photographs of various Lord Wardens and the Courts of Brotherhood and Guestling, the uniform of a baron who attended the coronation of George III and a piece of the canopy borne by him, and a tea-pot and cream-jug made from the silver of the canopy staves.

Here, at Rye, this short account of the Cinque Ports and Two Ancient Towns ends. Of their limbs, some of them as interesting, both historically and topographically, as their Head Ports, we have said little; the plan of this book made it impossible to deal with them according to their deserts, and they merit a volume to themselves.

THE SEAL OF THE BARONS OF OUR LORD
THE KING OF ENGLAND OF WINCHELSEA

The obverse of this Seal, temp.
Edward I, is 3½ inches in diameter.

INDEX

*The numerals in **heavy type** denote the figure number of the illustrations.*